The Elite Agent Handbook

The Proven Playbook for Attracting
Dream Clients, Selling Beautiful
Homes & Creating a Business
& Life You Love

Lucy & Michael Joerin

Foreword by Sarah Willingham

The Elite Agent Handbook
The Proven Playbook for Attracting Dream Clients, Selling Beautiful Homes & Creating a Business & Life You Love

© 2025 Stowhill Estates Limited

ISBN: 9781068169304 Paperback

Published by: Inspired By Publishing

The strategies in this book are presented primarily for enjoyment and educational purposes. Every effort has been made to trace copyright holders and obtain their permission for the use of copyright material.

To our beautiful children, Millie and Rose. You make every
day special just by being in it.

Love, Mum & Dad

xxx

In loving and grateful memory of our mentor and friend,
Sarah Edmundson, 1985-2024

"To laugh often and much; to win the respect of intelligent people and the affection of children; to earn the appreciation of honest critics and endure the betrayal of false friends; to appreciate beauty, to find the best in others; to leave the world a bit better, whether by a healthy child, a garden patch or a redeemed social condition; to know even one life has breathed easier because you have lived. This is to have succeeded."

– Bessie Anderson Stanley

Acknowledgements

Writing a book is not a solo mission. It takes a small (and sometimes sleep-deprived) army to bring it to life. We're endlessly grateful to everyone who has supported this project, from its inception to its appearance on the bookshelf.

First, to you, dear reader. Thank you for showing up, staying curious and being brave enough to believe there's a better way to do estate agency. We wrote this book for you, and it's a joy to know it's found its way into your hands.

To our families, including our parents, Chris, Brian, and Jenny, and our sisters and brothers-in-law, Cami, Jess, Tim and Dave. Thank you for your endless support, for cheering us on, celebrating with us and helping us hold our nerve when things got scary. We honestly couldn't have done this without you.

To our daughters, Millie and Rose, who inspire us every single day. Thank you for putting up with all the late nights, the interrupted holidays and the moments when work crept in where it shouldn't have. We hope we've shown you that you can be anything you want to be and that finishing something big is possible (even for us!). We love you more than words can say.

To Angela Haynes-Ranger, our brilliant Book Project Manager. Thank you for keeping us on track and for gently but effectively nudging us to actually finish this book (a small miracle, given our track record). Your clarity, patience and magic touch made all the difference.

To Sarah Turner, Amelia Turner and Jen Casey, our amazing Stowhill team. After all the hiring disasters (and you know there were a few), we finally got it right. You are the Dream Team in every sense: smart, committed, full of heart and humour. Thank you for going above and beyond – always – and for being such bloody great people. Please never leave. Seriously. We mean it.

To Sarah Willingham, our dear friend and Dragon. Thank you for graciously agreeing to write the foreword to this book and for championing ambitious entrepreneurs everywhere. Your support means the world to us.

To Conrad Zurini at Remax Escarpment in Canada. Thank you for championing us in the very early days and for your encouragement and belief when we were still finding our feet.

To our coaches and mentors, Sam Ashdown, Phil Jones, Ryan Pinnick, Nicola Lyle, Fabienne Fredrickson, Matt Elwell and Ned Shakir. Thank you for your wisdom, your generosity and for always knowing exactly what we needed to hear. And a thank you in particular, to Sarah Edmundson. You have no idea how much your support and encouragement meant to us, and we miss you desperately.

To our incredible industry friends, we are so lucky to work alongside such brilliant, kind and passionate people. You've inspired us, challenged us and made this journey so much richer. Special thanks to Georges Verdis, Julie Hill, John and Lisa Curran, Sara-May Smith, Michael Mortimer, Oliver and Danielle Gill, Julien Powell, Levi Fowler, David and Lottie Crooke, Simon Mackin, Fiona Wright and Benjamin Churchill. We're honoured to call you friends.

To our powerhouse Stowhill Franchise Partners, Tim and Jules (Berkshire), David and Sara (Buckinghamshire), Rosanagh and Dominic (Cheltenham), Rebecca Cooke (Hampshire) and Roberto Giambrone (Hertfordshire & N. Middlesex): You blow us away. Your ambition, integrity and commitment to excellence inspire us every single day. Watching you build incredible businesses and serve your communities at such a high level is one of the greatest privileges of our lives.

To our wonderful clients, those who took a punt on us in the early days, the ones who've become dear friends, and yes, even the nightmares (you know who you are). You've all shaped us, taught us, stretched us and helped us grow. Thank you for entrusting us with your homes and your stories. Special thanks to Mark and Vanessa Taylor – we're so grateful that you've turned from clients into dear friends. Thank you to Steve Bennett for believing in us and for supporting us when we most needed it. We will never forget your generosity.

And finally, to everyone who's ever whispered, "There must be a better way to do estate agency…" We hope this book helped you believe there is. Because there is. And you're holding it.

With love and deep gratitude,
Lucy & Michael

"It is not the critic who counts; not the man who points out how the strong man stumbles, or where the doer of deeds could have done them better. The credit belongs to the man who is actually in the arena, whose face is marred by dust and sweat and blood; who strives valiantly; who errs; who comes short again and again; who spends himself in a worthy cause; who at best knows in the end the triumph of high achievement, and who at the worst, if he fails, at least fails while daring greatly, so that his place shall never be with those cold and timid souls who neither know victory nor defeat."

– Theodore Roosevelt

Foreword

I first met Lucy back in 2007 when I was filming a BBC TV show called *The Restaurant* with Raymond Blanc. The show was somewhat akin to *The Apprentice* for restaurateurs. I was one of the judges, trying not to spill red wine down my top on camera, while Lucy was the PR dynamo behind the scenes, making sure I said all the right things.

Since then, Lucy and her brilliant husband Michael have become two of my favourite people. Over the years, I've watched them build a business with real heart, clear purpose and a proper plan. Let me tell you: That combination is rare. They've pushed boundaries and built something genuinely special in a world that, let's face it, hasn't always had the best reputation.

What they're doing with their business is changing the game in the estate agency industry. They're part of a movement to raise standards, redefine the industry and show clients what great service really looks like. And this book? Well, it's a breath of fresh air.

This isn't your typical "how to sell houses" book. It's not full of tired scripts or door-knocking tactics. It's a refreshing, honest and practical manual for building a high-end property business that actually works, without selling your soul or burning out in the process. And it's one that helps you sleep at night, too.

What sets it apart is the blend of mindset and strategy. That's the magic formula, in my opinion. You can have all the clever tools and shiny tactics in the world, but if your mindset's not right, if you don't believe in yourself or if you're still waiting for permission, you'll always stay stuck.

Lucy and Michael get this on a deep level. This book is like having them in your corner, cheering you on while quietly giving you all the trade secrets. It's as much about who you're becoming as it is about what you're doing. That's where the real transformation happens. This book is honest. It's practical. And it's written by two people who are in the trenches every day, living it, learning from it and now sharing it with you.

Since joining Dragons' Den, I've met hundreds of entrepreneurs. And you know what separates the truly great ones? It's not just the numbers or the pitch. It's the passion. The hunger to change something for the better. The depth of knowledge about their industry. And, crucially, the strength of the team they've built around them.

That's what you'll find in Lucy and Michael: a burning passion to raise the bar in estate agency, a deep understanding of what it takes to succeed in high-value homes and the kind of leadership that lifts everyone around them.

If you've ever dreamed of building your own business or breaking into a more lucrative, fulfilling part of the property world, let me say this: You absolutely can. You don't need to have gone to the right school. You don't need a double-barrelled surname. You just need a vision, a work ethic and the right support around you. That's exactly what this book offers. It will give you the mindset, the tools and the confidence to make it happen.

So read it. Take notes. Dog-ear the pages. But more importantly, take *action*.

Because success isn't reserved for the chosen few. It's there for anyone brave enough to back themselves. And if you're lucky enough to have Lucy and Michael as your guides, you're already ahead of the game.

Your dream is valid. And with the right support, the right mindset and the right strategy, you can build something brilliant.

Now go and make it happen.

Sarah Willingham

Entrepreneur, investor, founder and CEO of Nightcap

"If you want to see the future of Estate Agency, look at Michael & Lucy".

– Conrad Zurini, Remax Escarpment, Canada.

Contents

Introduction

Welcome to The Elite Agent Handbook. We want to be honest with you from the start: We never set out to become estate agents.

In fact, we've never met a child who says they want to grow up and be an estate agent. Astronaut, ballerina and footballer, sure. But, estate agent? Never. And honestly, we get it. The industry hasn't exactly done itself any favours. Shiny suits, dodgy sales tactics, zero customer service. It's no wonder estate agents regularly top the "least trusted profession" lists, somewhere between politicians and traffic wardens.

And yet, here we are: eight years in, 150+ high-value homes sold, multiple offices across some of the UK's most desirable postcodes and a thriving business that supports other ambitious agents to build their own high-fee, low-volume estate agency empires.

This book is the roadmap we wish we'd had when we started.

Back when we were sitting at our kitchen table with no experience, no listings and a vague dream of "selling really nice houses only." We had no idea how to sell a home – let alone a million-pound one – but we had a hunch that there must be a better way to run an estate agency. One that focused on quality over quantity, one that valued service and strategy over speed and spin. One where you don't need to hustle 24/7 just to scrape by.

The Industry Is Broken, But You Don't Have to Be

The average UK estate agent earns around £3,000 per deal. With fall-throughs, delays and bargain-basement fees, it's no surprise that most agents are stuck in a constant state of stress, burnout and underappreciation.

The current model rewards volume, not value. And the result? Exhausted agents, mediocre marketing and frustrated clients who wonder what exactly they're paying for.

But what if you could flip the script?

What if you could sell just one high-value home a month and earn £100,000+ a year, while working with dream clients who respect you, trust your advice and pay your fee without flinching?

We're here to tell you that it's not only possible; it's happening right now.

We've done it. Our partner agents are doing it. And in this book, we're going to show you exactly how.

Why We Wrote This Book

Over the last eight years, we've coached, mentored and masterminded hundreds of agents, new and experienced alike, and we kept hearing the same stories.

> "I don't know how to get into high-value homes."

> "I feel like I'm working all the time but not getting anywhere."

> "I'm great with clients, but I can't seem to get enough of the right ones."

> "I'm scared to charge more, even though I know I'm worth it."

> "I'm exhausted, and I miss seeing my kids."

Sound familiar?

We created *The Elite Agent Handbook* to change that.

This book serves as your blueprint for breaking free from the high-volume, low-fee trap. It's for agents who are tired of racing to the bottom, who want to serve at a higher level, and who are ready to build a business that supports their life, rather than the other way around.

Inside, you'll find the exact tools, systems, scripts, strategies and mindset shifts we used to go from total beginners to six-figure+ earners in the luxury homes market, which is exactly what we teach our franchise partners too.

And yes, we'll share our biggest wins, painful losses, face-palm mistakes and occasional moments of pure chaos, because real estate wouldn't be real without at least a *little* drama, right?

What You'll Learn

In these pages, you'll learn how to:

- Launch and grow a business that works for you, not just because of you
- Position yourself as the go-to expert in your niche
- Win listings, even when you're the highest fee and lowest valuation
- Build a predictable lead generation machine (without selling your soul on social media)
- Attract only your dream clients and gently repel the nightmares
- Market properties like luxury brands and stand out online
- Negotiate like a Ninja and justify your premium fee
- Create a business that pays you well, gives you time back and leaves you proud

You'll also get:

- Real-life stories from the trenches (some inspiring, some outrageous)
- Templates, frameworks and behind-the-scenes strategies
- A clear roadmap to get from where you are now to where you want to be

Who This Book Is For

This book is for you whether you're an experienced agent stuck in a volume-driven model, a corporate employee longing to go it alone or a complete newbie who's never sold a home before.

If you've ever dreamed of building a boutique agency, selling beautiful homes, commanding higher fees and working with people who light you up, this is your guide.

You don't need a silver tongue. You don't need a swanky office. You don't need 20 years of experience.

You need a system, a strategy and the mindset to go all in.

We wrote this book because we're passionate about raising the bar in estate agency. We do it every day in our business, Stowhill Estates, and we want to show you how you can do it too. Whether you're just starting out or you're an experienced agent ready to level up, this book is your roadmap. We hope you'll find it friendly, honest and packed with tips, tools and stories from the trenches.

We're here, ready to walk the journey with you. We've made mistakes and learned lessons (although we're still learning something new every day!). Now, we're sharing everything we know, so you don't have to learn the hard way.

Because here's the big secret:

You *can* build a successful, ethical and well-paid estate agency. You *can* serve your clients brilliantly and still have a life. And you *can* help transform the reputation of this industry, one beautiful home at a time

Final Word Before We Begin

This is not theory. It's not fluff. Everything in this book is tried, tested and used daily in our own business and by our partner agents across the UK.

So grab a notebook, pour yourself a coffee (or a glass of wine, we don't judge) and get ready to see estate agency in a whole new light.

Let's build the business you've been dreaming of.

It starts now.

Let's go.

Chapter 1
Why Does Everyone Hate Estate Agents?

The Reputation Problem and the Revolution Waiting to Happen

If you've ever cringed when telling someone what you do for a living, this book is for you.

If you've ever wished you could charge more, work less and serve better, this book is for you.

If you've ever felt that estate agency could be something more, something meaningful, respected and even joyful, then friend, you're in the right place.

Let's face it, estate agents get a bad rap. In the league of "least trusted professions," we're nestled somewhere between traffic wardens, politicians and advertising executives. Even *we* used to wince a little when we told someone at a dinner party what we did for a living. The polite smile. The barely concealed judgement. The awkward, "Oh, how interesting..." that followed.

And you know what? That reputation didn't just appear out of thin air. There's some truth in the public's perception, and that's precisely why we're writing this book. According to a recent Ipsos Veracity Index, only 37% of people trust estate agents to be truthful.

But here's the kicker: Estate agency is one of the most important professions in someone's life. You're helping people sell their biggest asset. You're guiding them through one of the most emotional, financially significant decisions they'll ever make.

So, how did such a vital role end up so universally disliked?

In this chapter, we will explore the truth behind the reputation, the broken system that created it and, more importantly, the incredible opportunity for those of us who want to do things differently. We'll share some horror stories, some hard truths and plenty of laughs. But most of all, we'll show you why you have the power to be part of the shift this industry desperately needs.

Michael's Story

I can't say I actively hate estate agents, but it's true I've never had much respect for the profession or even desired to be one. I know that sounds odd, given that I've built a million-pound business in the field.

I left school with few qualifications (though my woodwork O-level did come in handy, I'll admit!). After a stint as a Special Constable with Thames Valley Police, exploring whether law enforcement was the right path for me, I quickly realised that my strength lay in working with people from all walks of life. As a police officer, you often interact with people who don't exactly want to engage with you, so I found that a career in sales was a much better fit.

In the late 1980s, I completed an apprenticeship in cabinet and chair making, but I soon found myself drawn to the world of IT, a field I loved for the most part. In the later years, I ran a sales team across EMEA (Europe, Middle East and Africa) and APAC (Asia Pacific), travelling extensively, earning great money and meeting fantastic people. But as is common in corporate life, job security was never a given. After a restructuring here and a redundancy there, Lucy and I had a conversation, while watching yet another series of *Million Dollar Listing*, about taking our future into our own hands.

So, why estate agency? Well, Lucy's background is in PR and marketing, mine is in sales and we both share a love for property programmes. We'd always enjoyed watching Kevin McCloud's *Grand Designs* and any version of *Million Dollar Listing* we could find. We were also in the process of selling our home and looking at new properties when one agent, on a viewing, stayed on the doorstep and simply said, "I won't show you around, it is what it is." I turned to Lucy and said, "We could do this better!" She looked at me and replied, "Why don't we then?" And that's how Stowhill Estates was born.

A Model That's Not Working

The traditional UK estate agency model is built on volume. The more transactions, the better. The fees? Well, as we all know, they've been in a race to the bottom for years. But it wasn't always like this. Back in 2000, the average estate agent fee was close to 2%, but that number has been in steady decline for years and is now languishing around 1.4%, meaning that agents have to take on more stock just to stay afloat.

Agents are often juggling 20, 30 or even 50 listings at once, all for painfully modest commissions. The reality of this is long hours, missed weekends, constant stress and very little time to actually serve the people they're supposed to be helping.

Here are some sobering statistics: The average commission for a UK estate agent is currently £3780.00. On average, a house takes 185 days to sell (from listing to completion). That's a fee of around £20 per day per listing. Add to that our broken conveyancing system, and after all your hard work, your sale has a 1 in 4 chance of falling through. If, like most agents, you're a no-sale, no-fee agent, then you have a 25% chance of working 185 days for nothing, nada. In fact, it will have cost *you* money in terms of listing costs for Rightmove, putting together photos and other marketing materials and not to mention your time doing viewings and negotiating the sale.

It's no wonder the industry is held in such poor regard; it's also no wonder the public isn't thrilled with the level of service they receive from most estate agents. Overvalued properties, poor communication, rushed viewings and agents who disappear the moment a contract is signed. Sound familiar? And frankly, given the statistics, who can blame them?

If you're reading this as someone who is already working in estate agency, you might be nodding along. But here's the thing. You're not the problem. The model is. It's designed to keep agents on the hamster wheel, barely keeping the lights on, with little room to breathe (or eat lunch).

Now, when you tell family and friends that you're leaving a high-paying, well-respected IT career to become an "estate agent," you quickly find out what people think of the profession. But why such hostility to an essential service? Here are a few of the main reasons why.

The Reputation Problem

Ask the average person what they think of estate agents, and you'll get a mixture of eye rolls and horror stories. Pushy sales tactics. Misleading listings. Overpromising and underdelivering. A sharp suit and a sharper tongue.

And, fair enough, we've all met that agent. The one who rushes a family around a freezing cold home in 10 minutes flat. The one who tells the seller their house is worth £200,000 more than it actually is, just to win the listing. The one who ghosted the seller after promising "dozens of interested buyers" who apparently only existed in his imagination. Then there are the posh agents: the ones with tweed jackets, sporting gilets and names as long as their career titles, like Randolph von der Swashbuckle or Harriet Hammersmith-Flyover.

It's also true, though, that many people don't fully understand what an estate agent actually does to deserve their fee, because as an industry, we don't do a good enough job of showing how essential a good agent is to a stress-free sale at the maximum price.

Lack of Transparency

Some people feel that estate agents are less than transparent about the true condition or price of a property, pushing buyers or renters to make decisions quickly to secure a sale or lease. This, unsurprisingly, leads to general feelings of mistrust.

Pushy Sales Tactics

Estate agents, especially in a competitive market, can come across as too aggressive. This pushy behaviour can be off-putting, especially if people feel under pressure to make quick decisions.

Misleading Listings

Some estate agents advertise properties with exaggerated claims about size, features or location. When potential buyers or renters view the property, they may be disappointed or frustrated when the reality doesn't match the listing.

Personality Conflicts

In some cases, people simply don't get along with certain estate agents. It's a personality-driven industry, and some agents may come off as insincere, overly enthusiastic, or uninterested in the buyer's or seller's needs, leading to frustration.

We've encountered and heard all of these perspectives and behaviours. One particularly concerning case involved an agent whose contract, buried in the fine print, stated that their fee would be based on the marketing price of the home, not the final sale price. As a result, when the client accepted an offer below the asking price, the agent still charged a fee based on the original asking price.

Agents used to meet at the local pub to swap "war stories," but nowadays, it seems they're more focused on creating conflicts with one another. As one estate agent sales trainer once told us, "It's a contact sport."

As I write this, we are defending our position after recently winning an instruction from another agent. This agent is now claiming that they introduced a couple who initially saw the property online weeks ago when it was listed under their agency. However, the couple in question never contacted the first agent. Instead, they emailed the agent four days after the property was removed from the market, at which point their contract had expired, and we had already taken over as the exclusive listing agent. The former agent insists they introduced the couple and is demanding a fee if they decide to view and purchase the property. It's important to note that the couple never communicated with this agent, nor did they view the property while it was under their representation. Their contact occurred only after the previous agent's contract had expired and ours had already begun.

We've seen some truly unbelievable tactics from agents. One agent sent love heart emojis to clients of ours, clearly trying to build a "strong relationship" with them, only for the husband to ask, "What the hell is going on here?!" Needless to say, that agent didn't win the listing. In another instance, the same agent spread blatant lies, telling one of our clients that we were being sued over our company name. It was completely false.

Another agent we're familiar with employs a rather questionable tactic of telling buyers there are so many offers that the property will go to sealed bids. This artificially inflates the price, benefiting the sellers but being incredibly unfair to the buyers, especially when we discovered that, on more than one occasion, there was only ever one offer on the table.

One of our friends, who was selling outside our area (and not through us), had an agent claim that they'd conducted 15 viewings in one day. However, thanks to a "nanny cam" in the house, our friend discovered that no one had actually shown up!

So, agents don't exactly help their own cause, to be honest. It's an unregulated sector, and perhaps it should be more tightly controlled. After all, you're entrusting your agent with what is typically your largest financial asset.

Let's Flip It

We're sorry if we've depressed you so far. But we do have some good news. There is a better way. A model that puts the client first allows you, as the agent, to offer a world-class service and – wait for it – actually makes you decent money!

It starts by turning the old volume-driven system on its head. Instead of chasing dozens of low-fee listings, what if you focused instead on fewer, high-value homes? What if you charged a proper fee for a premium service, and actually had the time and energy to deliver it?

This is how we built our agency, Stowhill Estates. We specialise in selling beautiful and unique homes at £1m and above. And we have only ever specialised in selling at this level. Honestly, we've had some backlash in the past from some old-school agents who felt we ought to have "earned our stripes" in the volume-based high-street model or by working as an employee for a dusty old corporate agency. But frankly, we had no interest in trying against the odds to build a profitable business based on a broken model, and besides, who has time for that anyway? Why learn from an outdated and broken way of doing things only to have to unlearn it all to try a better way?

In our business, who we say "no" to is as important (and maybe even more important) than who we say "yes" to. We're not trying to list every home. Instead, we work with a smaller number of hand-picked clients (yes, we pick them as much as they pick us) who want and deserve a much more personal, concierge home-selling service. That means more time for marketing. More time for negotiation. More time for *people*. And a better outcome for everyone.

Why High-Value Homes?

If you've ever thought about moving into the high-value homes market but felt it was out of reach, this part's for you.

You might imagine that this space is dominated by posh, pinky-ringed, double-barrelled surname types who went to the right schools and say things like "frightfully good" without irony. But the truth is, it really isn't, we promise.

The luxury market is changing, and fast. The owners of unique and beautiful homes these days are entrepreneurs and CEOs, not the landed gentry. Clients at this level don't care where you went to school. Instead, they care about results. They care about service. They care about how well you understand their needs and how expertly you can guide them through the process.

This isn't about being flashy, it's about being *excellent*.

And the beauty about this end of the market? People expect to pay more for your time, strategy and expertise. You're not just a middleman anymore. You're a trusted advisor. A marketing expert. A negotiation pro. A steady hand in what is often an emotional and high-stakes process.

The fees are higher. The expectations are higher. But so are the rewards.

This means that you can work with fewer clients, deliver a truly exceptional experience and still earn a brilliant living. In fact, you might even work less and earn more. Imagine that!

Yes, the stakes are higher, but so is the satisfaction. And when you get it right, you'll build the kind of reputation that has clients referring you again and again.

Why DIY Doesn't Work

Remember when Purple Bricks first came on the scene? Their promises of low (or no) fees and total control for sellers sounded revolutionary and had many established agents seriously worried. But somewhere along the way, the wheels fell off.

The company, once valued at over £1 billion, has never made a profit in its history, despite spending around £27m per year on advertising. In 2023, Purple Bricks was sold for £1. That's not a typo. *One pound.*

Why? Because DIY might work for flat-pack furniture, but it doesn't work for selling someone's biggest financial asset. There's simply too much at stake. People want guidance. They want expertise. And more than anything, they want someone who *cares*.

Selling a home should never feel like a DIY job. It should feel like a first-class experience. From staging to strategy, from negotiation to completion, you need someone holding your hand the whole way.

The Future Is Independent

In countries such as Australia and the USA, as well as some European countries, estate agencies already look quite different. The top agents run their own independent businesses under a brokerage model. They build strong personal brands, and they charge proper fees. They offer a high-touch, full-service experience that clients rave about.

This is where we believe the UK estate agency is heading – and not before time! It's where we believe it should head. Because the more fantastic independent agents there are, the higher the standards we'll set for the entire industry. And when standards rise, so do fees, reputations and results.

Think about it. If you're being paid really well for fewer transactions, you can hire brilliant staff, invest in fantastic marketing and genuinely go above and beyond for your clients. That's good for you, and it's great for your clients. Everyone wins.

Independent agents are already starting to take over the property world, and we're championing them all the way. And not the old-school, shiny-suited stereotype. We're talking modern, savvy, passionate professionals who genuinely care about people and property.

And the best part? There's space for you here.

With the rise of independent, boutique agencies and the growing influence of US practices, where brokers are highly trained, licensed, customer-focused, and respected in their field, we're starting to see and actively drive a shift in how estate agents are perceived in the UK. In the US, you may often have a "broker for life," and we're gradually moving in that direction here.

Our focus is on delivering an exceptional customer experience for both sellers and buyers, offering bespoke marketing, transparency and incredible integrity. And it's working.

We believe the larger corporate agencies (the dinosaurs of the industry) are being seriously challenged and will continue to struggle unless they evolve. As sellers realise they have more options, they will increasingly choose the independent agent: the one who only earns when they sell your home and delivers top-tier service and marketing to get the best results.

Let's Make It an Experience!

We believe moving house should be exciting, emotional and even joyful. Not just a transaction to tick off.

Let's be real for a minute. Yes, it's stressful. Yes, it can be complicated. But it's also a huge moment in someone's life. That deserves more than a 10-minute valuation, a few photos taken with an iPhone and a "good luck" handshake!

Our mission is to make the home-selling process feel more like buying a luxury car than filling out a parking permit. Tailored, attentive, and, dare we say it, fun!

Here are some of the key initiatives that we, alongside other like-minded independent agents, are implementing to improve and enhance our industry:

Greater Transparency

Clear communication. We are committed to providing comprehensive information about properties, the buying or renting process and the associated fees. This includes clear explanations at each stage of the transaction, along with honest assessments of properties – no exaggeration.

Honest pricing. Transparency in pricing is essential. By clearly outlining fees, commissions and pricing structures, we help buyers and sellers avoid frustration, foster trust and ensure that expectations are met.

Ethical Standards & Regulation

Stricter oversight. Increased industry regulation can ensure that agents adhere to a clear code of conduct, promoting professionalism and minimising bad practices.

Promoting best practices. We are committed to ethical standards that prioritise client needs. Rather than pushing for quick sales, we aim to assist clients with responsible, fair and transparent transactions.

Customer-Centric Approach

Personalised service. We put client needs first. Instead of rushing clients into decisions, we take time to understand their preferences and provide tailored options that truly meet their needs.

Relationship building. Estate agents should not only focus on transactions. By cultivating trust through meaningful relationships and offering positive experiences, whether or not they result in a sale, we help foster long-term client satisfaction and referrals.

Showcasing Expertise & Value

Knowledge sharing. We aim to position ourselves as trusted advisors, offering valuable market insights, tips on buying or renting and guidance on the local area. This transforms the perception of agents from salespeople to experts dedicated to informed decision-making.

Emphasising value over fees. We focus on the value we provide, not just commissions. This includes guiding clients through paperwork, negotiating favourable deals and offering access to exclusive properties not available elsewhere.

Transparent Fee Structures

Fair and clear fees. To address concerns about high or hidden fees, we advocate for transparent fee structures that clearly outline all applicable charges. Fixed fees can often feel more justifiable than percentage-based commissions, particularly in high-value markets.

Demonstrating value for fees. We ensure that our fees accurately reflect the tangible value we offer, whether that's negotiating a better price, managing legal processes, or providing additional post-sale services.

Leveraging Technology

Modern tools. By incorporating cutting-edge technology, such as virtual tours, automated updates and user-friendly platforms, we make the buying and selling process more efficient for both clients and agents.

Responsive communication. Timely responses through multiple communication channels (email, phone, text) demonstrate our commitment to valuing clients' time and providing the best customer experience.

Positive PR & Branding

Public relations campaigns. We actively promote stories of success and go-beyond client service to counter negative stereotypes and showcase our commitment to helping clients.

Client testimonials and reviews. Highlighting authentic, positive feedback is crucial. Real client stories help build trust and demonstrate that estate agents can be reliable and trustworthy partners.

Effective & Honest Marketing

Authentic listings. We take pride in accurately representing properties in all our marketing materials. High-quality images and honest descriptions ensure that clients are never misled by exaggerated or misleading content.

Educational content. Offering informative blogs, videos and resources empowers clients. By demonstrating our knowledge and expertise, we move beyond being mere salespeople to trusted guides throughout the process.

Addressing Industry-Wide Issues

Tackling supply and demand challenges. In areas with housing shortages, estate agents can be seen as part of the issue. We advocate for policy changes, promote affordable housing and engage in meaningful discussions to improve the overall housing landscape.

Community Engagement

Giving back. We believe in supporting our local communities by sponsoring events, backing local charities and contributing to sustainability initiatives. Our focus goes beyond sales to improving the broader community.

Educational seminars. Hosting free seminars or webinars for first-time buyers or renters positions us as knowledgeable and caring professionals, eager to share expertise and guide individuals through their real estate journey.

Watch this space, or better yet, join the movement to make it happen!

You Are the Revolution

Independent agents *will* take over the property world.

Those who build personal brands, deliver concierge-level service and get paid properly because they're worth it. Those who make clients feel seen, heard and valued. The future belongs to you. And there's plenty of room at the top.

We wrote this chapter not to moan, but to motivate. Because once you see how broken the system is, you'll also see the opportunity to build something better.

You can be part of the new wave of agents: modern, ethical, independent and damned good at what you do. You can set a new standard for what estate agency looks and feels like.

You can be the reason someone trusts estate agents again.

And that? Well, that's a reputation worth having.

Chapter 2
The Mindset of the
Elite Agent

The Unseen Edge: Why the Best Agents Start With Mindset, Not Marketing

Before we delve into the practical strategies for becoming an Elite Agent, we need to address something that underpins everything: your mindset.

Now, we get it, "mindset" can sound a bit woo-woo. But hang in there. Because the truth is, strategy alone isn't enough. If you're subconsciously sabotaging your own success, no amount of clever tactics will get you the results you want.

Before you skip ahead, give us 20 minutes and an open mind. We promise that this is the part that makes all the difference.

What Do We Mean by "Mindset"?

Mindset is simply the lens through which you view the world. It's made up of your beliefs, assumptions and inner narratives and it shapes everything: how you think, feel, act and, ultimately, succeed.

Here's the mind-blowing bit: Over 95% of your decisions are made unconsciously. Let that sink in. Most of the time, you're not in the driver's seat. As Carl Jung put it, "Until you make the unconscious conscious, it will direct your life, and you will call it fate."

Your subconscious is running the show. And unless you actively work with it, it will keep following a script you didn't write.

Think about it: How much time have you spent learning strategy, versus learning to reprogram your unconscious mind?

Business is only just beginning to catch up with the science on this. But we believe that in a few years, understanding mindset won't be "out there." Instead, it'll be standard. Not in a fluffy "think positive" way but in a grounded, neuroscience-backed way.

At our agency, mindset mastery isn't optional – it's core. We coach our agents to adopt what we call the "Millionaire Agent Mindset." And no, it's not just about money. It's about abundance – in love, joy, freedom, knowledge and, yes, financial success too, if that's what you want.

How Your Brain Actually Works

Let's break this down simply, no neuroscience degree required.

Your brain has two key players:

The conscious mind (your logical, goal-driven "Einstein" brain).

The subconscious mind (your fast, emotional, safety-obsessed "Frankenstein" brain).

Your Einstein brain dreams big. It makes plans, sets goals and gets excited about the future.

Your Frankenstein brain? It just wants to keep you safe. And it has been programmed, mostly during childhood, by parents, teachers, the media and life experiences. Its job is protection, not progress. It clings to what's familiar, even if it holds you back.

These two minds often conflict. You say you want to scale your income or raise your fees, but your subconscious whispers:

"You're not good enough."

"What if you fail?"

"People like you don't earn that kind of money."

And suddenly, without realising it, you're procrastinating, self-sabotaging or feeling mysteriously exhausted.

How Limiting Beliefs Show Up

Ever experienced these?

- Feeling tired or unmotivated for no clear reason
- Financial success on paper, but a nagging sense of dissatisfaction
- A growing to-do list that feels like Mt. Everest
- Constant procrastination on the one thing that would move the needle
- Toxic clients who don't respect your time or expertise
- Money that slips through your fingers as fast as it comes in

These are all signs of subconscious sabotage.

Your subconscious wants to keep you in your comfort zone, and it's sneaky. It convinces you you're just tired, or "being realistic" or that now just isn't the right time.

We've been there. We've felt all of it.

Our Story: Success Without Fulfilment

When we started our business, we focused entirely on the practical stuff. We followed the training to the letter, hit big milestones and by year three, we had our best financial year yet.

But we were exhausted. Burned out. Strangely unfulfilled.

We were doing "all the right things," yet everything felt like a slog. Clients were rude or demanding. Cash flow was patchy. Sales would fall through. Staff weren't working out. And the joy had evaporated.

The business wasn't broken. *We* were.

Or, more accurately, our subconscious beliefs were.

Then COVID hit. With life on pause, we finally had time to reflect – and to read. What started with books on resilience soon turned into a deep dive into mindset, neuroscience and subconscious programming.

And everything changed.

Where Do Limiting Beliefs Come From?

Most of our deepest beliefs are formed before the age of seven, when our brains are in a super-receptive, meditative "Alpha" state. At that age, we're like little sponges, soaking up every message from our parents, caregivers, teachers, peers and media.

We're not blaming your parents (love you, Mum and Dad!), but it helps to understand where these beliefs come from. Messages like:

"You have to work hard to succeed."

"Money doesn't grow on trees."

"Rich people are greedy."

"Who do you think you are?"

Over time, these messages become your internal blueprint, the rules your subconscious follows without question.

So, even when your conscious mind says, "I want to be financially free," your subconscious says, "Freedom equals risk." And bam – you sabotage yourself.

The Inner Conflict: Einstein vs Frankenstein

Let's say you decide to leave your safe corporate job to start your dream estate agency.

Your Einstein brain lights up:

"Imagine the freedom, the income, the impact I'll have!"

But your Frankenstein brain fires back:

"What if you fail?"

"Remember the last time something didn't work out?"

"You'll lose everything."

This voice can be brutal. And it sounds like *you*, which makes it even more convincing.

When your brain is in conflict, the subconscious almost always wins. Not because it's right, but because it's faster, louder and laser-focused on keeping you safe (read: stuck).

That's why so many talented people settle for mediocrity. But you don't have to.

Reprogramming Your Mindset: 7 Steps to Rewire for Success

Here's the great news: Just like a computer, your brain can be reprogrammed. Here's how to install new, empowering beliefs, ones that *actually* support your goals.

1. Recognise and Name the Limiting Belief

Awareness is the first step.

Ask yourself:

> "What belief is holding me back?"
>
> "Where did I learn this?"
>
> "Is it 100% true for every person, in every situation?"

Write it down. Challenge it. Replace it.

Example: "People won't pay my fee."

Rewrite it: "People happily pay for expertise and personal service."

2. Craft a New Empowering Belief

Choose a belief that feels like a stretch, but is still believable.

Example: "I don't have enough experience."

Rewrite it: "My fresh approach is exactly what modern sellers want."

Stick it on your mirror, your lock screen or wherever you'll see it daily.

3. Visualise and Feel Your Success

Your subconscious speaks in pictures and emotions.

Each morning, close your eyes and feel:

Walking confidently into a dream listing.

Quoting your fee and hearing "Yes!"

Seeing your income goal hit in your bank account.

Create a vivid "mental movie trailer" and play it daily.

4. Use Emotion-Driven Affirmations

Say affirmations out loud with conviction and emotion:

"I am a high-value agent. My service changes lives."

"I attract clients who appreciate and pay me well."

"Every day I grow more aligned with success."

Bonus: Record them in your voice and play them during your commute.

5. Catch Yourself in the Act

When fear creeps in, catch it mid-thought: "That's the old me. The new me honours my worth."

Create a physical anchor, like pressing your thumb and forefinger together, and pair it with a phrase like, "I've got this."

6. Build a Morning Mindset Ritual

Just like physical training, this is daily work.

Try this 10-minute routine:

- 3 minutes of gratitude journaling
- 5 minutes of visualisation
- 2 minutes of affirmations
- 1 power question: "How can I serve at a higher level today?"

Set a reminder. Make it non-negotiable.

7. Surround Yourself With Growth-Minded People

Mindset is contagious. Choose your circle wisely.

Connect with agents who charge premium fees.

Join a mastermind that normalises abundance.

Curate your social media feed to inspire, not drain you.

These are just some small ways you can start to surround yourself with like-minded people.

This Is the Work That Changes Everything

If you've read this far, you've already done the hardest bit: You've become *aware*.

Most people stop here. They nod, they agree, they highlight a few lines… and then they go back to the same patterns.

But not you.

You picked up this book because you're ready. You're ready to stop outsourcing your self-worth to the market, your competitors or your past and start backing yourself, fully.

Will it be easy? No.

Will it be worth it? Hell yes.

When you commit to mastering your mindset:

You walk into a £2 million home like you belong there – because you do.

You quote your full fee with confidence – because you know your value.

You attract dream clients – because you finally respect yourself first.

So here's our challenge: Don't just read this chapter. Live it.

Rewire the belief. Start the ritual. Raise your fee. Walk away from that energy-sucking client.

The version of you who already has the success you want? They've done this work.

They're waiting for you on the other side of your next brave step.

You are not your thoughts. You are the thinker of your thoughts. You can also choose new ones at any time.

Choose the ones that make you unstoppable.

You're already halfway there.

Now go. Build your mindset. Build your business.

Let's change this industry one brilliant, joyful, high-performing agent at a time.

Chapter 3
Built on Purpose

*How to Define Your Vision, Mission and Values
and Build a Business That Feels Like You*

When most estate agents go out on their own, they start with the practical aspects: business cards, a logo, possibly a website and a Rightmove account. They focus on listings, leads and how to make the phone ring. And that makes sense, as those things feel urgent. However, what often gets overlooked is the *foundational* work: taking the time to clarify your vision, mission and values. And it's a costly mistake.

Why? Because when things get busy (and they will), or when things get tough (and they will), you need more than grit. You need a compass. Something that helps you stay focused on why you started, who you serve and how you want to build, not just what you want to earn. Without that clarity, it's easy to say yes to the wrong clients, follow someone else's version of success or burn out chasing goals that don't even light you up.

Full disclosure: It took us a couple of years in business before we sat down and defined our vision, mission and values. But when we did, it was game-changing. It was probably because when we started Stowhill Estates at our kitchen table, neither of us really believed it would turn into the business it has. We were just "trying out estate agency." But once we got super-clear on our vision and focused on our mission, everything changed in our business – and in our personal lives, too. Suddenly, it felt like we had a purpose, a compass to direct our actions. It felt like there was real meaning to our work.

Your vision, mission and values are not just feel-good words; they're your north star. They guide your decisions, shape your brand, attract the right clients and help you build a business that actually feels like you. They really do give your work meaning, and meaning is what will keep you going when motivation wears thin.

As leadership expert Simon Sinek famously said, "People don't buy what you do; they buy why you do it." And in the world of high-value homes, where trust, alignment and emotional connection are everything, this couldn't be more true. Your vision, mission and values are not just internal business tools – they're the foundation of your brand identity.

They give clients a reason to choose you, not because you're the cheapest or the closest, but because your why resonates with theirs. When you can clearly communicate what you stand for and where you're going, you attract clients who believe what you believe. That's when a business stops feeling like a hustle and starts to feel like a calling.

This chapter is your invitation to slow down before you speed up. To step back and take a broader view. It's about setting your intention: not just to build a business, but to build the *right* business. One that aligns with your life, your purpose and your personal definition of success.

Let's begin.

Section 1: Creating Your Vision

Start with the end in mind, and make it worth building.

Your vision is your destination. It's the big picture. The future you're building towards, not just in your business, but in your life. It's where you're headed in 3, 5 or even 10 years' time. And yet, most estate agents don't have a clearly defined one. They have vague goals ("sell more homes", "make six figures") but not a real vision. And without a clear destination, it's incredibly easy to get lost, or worse, end up somewhere you never actually wanted to be.

Creating your vision is about getting intentional. It's about lifting your head from the daily grind and asking:

"What kind of business do I want to run?"

"What kind of life do I want to live?"

"How do I want to feel as I build it?"

Don't just think in numbers; think in experiences. What kind of clients are you working with? How many hours a week are you working? What does your role look like? Are you building a solo brand, a boutique team or a business that runs without you? Are you working from a home office or walking into your own beautiful high-street premises with a team that energises you?

This is your opportunity to imagine without limits. To design your business around your life and not the other way around.

Vision Is Personal (and It Should Be)

Your vision doesn't need to impress anyone else. It doesn't have to match what other agents are doing. Some people want a £1 million business and a large team. Others want to work three days a week with just five amazing clients and have Fridays off for long lunches and life admin. There's no wrong answer – only what's right for you.

If you skip this step, you risk defaulting to someone else's version of success and wondering why it doesn't feel good once you get there.

Exercise: Future You

Take 15 minutes and write a journal entry as if it's 3 years from now. Write it in the present tense.

"It's April 2028, and I'm sitting at my kitchen table with a coffee, reflecting on how far I've come…"

Describe your business. Your income. Your clients. Your lifestyle. How you feel day-to-day. The kind of agent you've become. Don't overthink it; just let the vision flow.

When you're done, go back through it and highlight what really matters to you. What themes emerge? What would feel truly exciting, fulfilling and aligned?

That's your vision.

Why It Matters

Once your vision is clear, everything else gets easier. You can reverse-engineer your strategy. You know what to say yes to and what to walk away from. You stop chasing other people's goals and start building something that's deeply aligned with your values, your strengths and your lifestyle.

You've now set your destination. The rest of this chapter is about plotting your route.

Section 2: Crafting Your Mission

Define why your business exists beyond just making sales.

If your vision is the destination, your mission is the engine. It's the reason your business exists, beyond just making money or "selling homes." It captures the difference you want to make, the kind of people you want to help and the way you want to help them. It's your purpose, and in this business, purpose sells.

Most agents lack a clear mission. Or if they do, it's some generic line like, "We provide excellent customer service," which sounds good but means nothing. A great mission doesn't just describe what you do; it speaks directly to the heart of your ideal client. It shows them that you get them, that you care and that you're here to make a meaningful impact.

Why Your Mission Matters

When you're clear on your mission, you:

- Attract clients who align with your values
- Know what to say no to
- Stand out from other agents who are all saying the same things
- Feel more inspired, especially on the hard days

It also anchors your brand. Your tone of voice, marketing style, fee justification and service model can all flow from your mission. And when you and your clients believe in the same "why," you're no longer just another agent; they see you as their trusted advisor.

Creating Your Own Mission Statement

A mission statement is a short, powerful summary that captures the essence of your business: what you do, who you do it for and why it matters. It's not a slogan or a fluffy marketing phrase; it's a guiding declaration of your purpose and values. Think of it as the compass for your decisions, team culture and client experience. A good mission statement should be concise, one to three sentences maximum, yet meaningful enough to inspire you and anyone who reads it. The goal is clarity, not complexity. If you can't explain your mission in a few lines, you probably aren't clear on it yourself. Keep it specific, grounded and true to your brand's voice.

A simple formula you can start with is:

We help [who] achieve [what], by [how].

Here are a few examples:

"We help discerning homeowners sell their unique homes for maximum value, through beautiful bespoke marketing and exceptional service."

"We help families find the perfect forever home by listening deeply, negotiating confidently, and putting people before property."

"We help time-poor professionals sell with ease, clarity, and a touch of calm, so they can focus on life, not logistics."

Make it specific. Make it real. Make it *you*.

A Mission That Resonates

Your mission should light you up. It should remind you why you do this work and help you stay grounded when you're dealing with tricky clients, slow markets or solicitor-induced migraines. It's also something your clients should *feel* in every interaction, from your first valuation to the moment you hand over the keys. Your mission becomes the heartbeat of your business.

Next, let's explore how your values shape how you show up and deliver on your mission.

Section 3: Clarifying Your Values

Your vision is where you're going. Your mission is why you do what you do. Your values are how you do it, and who you are while you're doing it.

Your values are your filter. Use them to build a business you're proud of.

In a world where "good service" is claimed by every agent and "integrity" is just a bullet point on a pitch, your values have to go deeper than vague statements. They should be lived, not laminated. That means they show up in the way you answer the phone, the tone of your emails, how you handle conflict and how you treat people when no one's watching.

Think of your values as the culture of your business, even if it's just you right now. They're the invisible code that guides every decision you make: who you work with, how you market, how you price and how you show up in tough moments.

What Do Values Actually Look Like?

Values don't have to be formal or corporate. In fact, the more authentically *you* they are, the more powerful they'll be.

Some examples of meaningful, actionable values:

Clarity over fluff. We speak plainly, honestly and never hide behind jargon.

Beauty matters. We believe homes deserve to be presented with care, detail and style.

People first, always. We put our client's peace of mind before our commission.

Professional, not pushy. We guide with confidence, not pressure.

We don't ghost. Our clients never have to chase us. We over-communicate – on purpose.

Here are our Stowhill Estates values:

Integrity. We do the right thing, even when no one is watching, and take radical responsibility.

Authenticity. We understand that people perform better when they can be their true selves.

Dynamic. We bring energy, creativity and imagination to our work.

Team. We value, support and respect one another. We raise each other up.

Driven. We are determined and focused on reaching our goals.

Fun. We don't take ourselves too seriously, and we take time to celebrate our success.

These are the kinds of values that differentiate you, not because you say them, but because you live them.

Exercise: Define Your Core Values

Take 10–15 minutes to reflect on the following:

What behaviours are non-negotiable in your business?

What do you admire in others you trust?

What do you *never* want a client to feel when working with you?

When are you most proud of how you handled something?

From here, choose 5 to 7 core values that feel true to you. Then, for each one, write a sentence about how that value shows up in action. This becomes your internal code – and your external brand promise.

Tip: You can share these with your clients as part of your onboarding or proposal pack. It sets a powerful tone from the very start.

When you're clear on your values, your confidence grows, your decisions become easier and your brand becomes magnetic. You attract clients who *get it*, and more importantly, who get *you*.

Ready to put it all together? In the next section, we'll show you how to bring your vision, mission and values to life in your brand, business and everyday actions.

Section 4: Aligning Vision, Mission & Values in Practice

This is how you turn clarity into confidence and confidence into clients.

You've defined your vision for the future you want to build. You've written your mission statement, the purpose behind what you do. And you've clarified your values, the way you'll show up every day. Now what?

Now, you align.

It's not enough to have a beautifully written statement tucked away in a notebook or stuck on your office wall. Vision, mission and values only become powerful when they are lived. When they shape your brand, your behaviour and your business decisions.

Use Them to Make Decisions

When you're clear on these three things, you stop second-guessing yourself. You can ask:

"Does this new instruction align with my vision for the business I want to build?"

"Does this marketing campaign reflect my mission?"

"Is this client a values match or a red flag?"

When the answer is no, you walk away. When the answer is yes, you go all in.

This clarity becomes your filter for everything, from who you work with to how you price, how you hire and even what content you share on social media. No more chasing every opportunity. Just intentional growth in the right direction.

Let It Shape Your Brand

Your vision, mission and values shouldn't just live in your head; they should be felt by everyone who comes into contact with your business. That means weaving them into your website and marketing copy, referencing them in client consultations and pitch decks or sharing stories that demonstrate them in action (e.g. how you handled a tricky negotiation or delivered something unexpected for a client)

When your values are visible, they become a magnet for the right clients and a subtle deterrent to the wrong ones.

Embed Them in Your Culture

Even if you're a solo agent right now, this is your culture in the making. As you grow your team or collaborate with others, these principles become the foundations of how you hire, delegate and lead.

If you want to build a business that feels good to run, you have to make it clear what you stand for and then hold yourself (and your team) to that standard.

When vision, mission and values are aligned, you stop trying to prove yourself and start showing up *as* yourself. You stop competing on price and start standing out on purpose. You build a business that not only delivers results but also feels fulfilling, sustainable and uniquely yours.

Section 5: Bringing It to Life

Your vision, mission and values are only powerful when you act on them.

Now that you've done the deep thinking – defining where you're going, why you're doing it and how you want to show up – it's time to take that clarity and bring it into the real world.

This is where you turn a thoughtful reflection into a visible identity. A private intention into a public brand. A personal mission to a profitable business. When you start building with this level of intention, people feel it. Clients trust it. And your business becomes something you're proud of – not just because it earns well, but because it feels aligned with your values.

Create a One-Page Business Manifesto

Pull together your vision, mission and values into a clear, visual document. Something you can look at daily to remind yourself of who you are and where you're going. This can be for your eyes only or something you share with clients and collaborators.

Include:

- Your 3- to 5-year vision (written in present tense)
- Your mission statement
- 5 to 7 core values, each with a sentence on how it shows up in your work

This document becomes your personal North Star and a tool to recalibrate when things get noisy or messy (which they will).

Let It Shape Your Marketing & Messaging

Use this clarity to refine your:

- Website copy
- Social media tone of voice
- Brand visuals
- Listing presentations
- Email signature
- Client onboarding documents

When all your touchpoints are infused with the same energy and message, your brand becomes magnetic. You attract people who align with you and repel those who don't (which is a blessing, not a problem).

Revisit, Refine, Repeat

This work isn't something you do once and forget about. As your business grows, your life evolves and your confidence deepens, your vision may shift. That's okay. Great businesses evolve.

Make a point to check in with your vision, mission and values at least once a year. Ask yourself, "Does this still feel true? Am I living this? Where have I drifted? What do I need to recommit to or let go of?"

You didn't go into business just to work harder. You went into business to build something meaningful, something with purpose, something *better* for yourself, your family and your clients.

Success With Soul

Building a business without a clear vision, mission and values is like trying to navigate without a map. You might make progress, but it's easy to lose direction, drift off course or end up somewhere that doesn't feel quite right. This work is foundational. It's what separates agents who build reactive, exhausting businesses from those who create purposeful, aligned and profitable ones. And in the premium homes market, this matters even more.

When you're working at the top end of the property ladder, your clients expect more than just efficiency and good service. They're looking for leadership, clarity and intention. They want to know who you are, what you stand for and whether they can trust you with one of their most valuable assets. That trust doesn't come from a slick logo or a polished pitch; it comes from being consistent, values-led and totally aligned with your message.

Your vision shows clients where you're headed. Your mission tells them why you do what you do. And your values show them exactly what kind of experience they can expect when they work with you.

This isn't just how you attract the right clients. It's how you build a business you actually love. One that grows sustainably, earns generously and reflects who you are, not just what you do.

So take the time to do this work. Revisit it often. Let it guide your next step and every step after that. Because when you build a business that feels like you, success doesn't just happen. It becomes inevitable.

Head to the Resources section at the back of this book to download your free Vision, Mission and Values worksheet.

Chapter 4
The Power of You: Building a Personal Brand That Sells

How to Stand Out, Win Trust and Charge What You're Worth

Your reputation precedes you, so make sure it reflects everything you want it to.

If you're in the high-value homes market, you're not just selling properties – you're selling trust, expertise and reputation. And in a world where clients Google you before they call you, your personal brand is either working for you or against you.

Gone are the days when a glossy brochure and a swanky office were enough. Today's high-net-worth clients want more. They want a face, a story, a personality. They want to know who you are, what you stand for and whether they can trust you with their most valuable asset. And they make that decision long before you step over the threshold.

This chapter is designed to help you take control of your narrative. To be known not just for *what* you do, but *how* you do it and most importantly, *why* you do it that way. We'll walk you through the nuts and bolts of personal branding: how to define it, build it, communicate it and use it to win more instructions, charge higher fees and build a business that feels as good as it looks.

Because in this market, it's not enough to be the best. You have to be seen as the best. And that's where your personal brand comes in.

You've probably seen and heard top entrepreneurs and business leaders talking about the importance of building a "personal brand," but what is it, why is it important and how do you go about building your own?

In this chapter, we'll look at this in more detail, as well as share with you some actionable steps you can implement straight away to start crafting your personal brand and elevating your visibility.

One of our mentors, Phil Jones, who co-founded Ashdown Jones in the Lake District, told us that when he first started his agency, his super-fancy website went live and he expected the phone to start ringing straight away. When it didn't, he was checking the phone lines, convinced that there was some error with the phone system! As it turned out, there was nothing wrong with his phone line; at the time, he just hadn't built up a strong enough personal brand to attract clients to him. He was expecting the website to do all the heavy lifting by itself, although we're happy to say that has completely changed now, and Phil and his agency are probably the best-known experts in the high-value homes area of the Lake District.

So what exactly is personal branding and why does it matter so much in business, especially in estate agency?

Let's break it down.

Personal Branding Isn't Just Marketing

Personal branding isn't just marketing; it's your identity in the marketplace.

At its core, personal branding is the process of defining, developing and communicating the unique combination of skills, experience, personality and values that only you can bring to your clients. It's what people say about you when you're not in the room, and it's the feeling that your brand evokes.

For estate agents operating in the ultra-competitive high-value homes space, your personal brand can become your most powerful differentiator. In a market where every agent says they're "passionate about property" and provides "world-class customer service," your brand is what sets you apart from the sea of sameness.

Why Does It Matter?

Well, put simply, high-value clients are unlikely to choose an agent based solely on the agency brand or the fee you charge, so a race to the bottom and charging less than your competitors is unlikely to win you the instruction on its own. Plus, you risk damaging your reputation if you only compete on fee.

High-value homeowners choose based on trust, credibility and reputation. Your personal brand is the bridge between visibility and trust. It's what positions you as an authority and helps potential clients feel confident when putting one of their most valuable assets in your hands. In the high-value homes market, trust is the currency. Your potential clients don't just want an agent; they want an expert. Someone who understands their world, who gets them results and with whom they feel confident.

When built well, a personal brand will help you:

- Effortlessly attract your ideal clients
- Consistently command higher fees (even help you win against other agents charging less!)
- Create influence and build a reputation, opening doors to more opportunities
- Build long-term client loyalty and generate consistent referrals
- Set you apart from your competition
- Empower you to be in control of who you wish to work with

Personal Brand vs Business Brand

You might be wondering, "What's the difference between your personal brand and a business brand?"

Think of your business brand as the company's public-facing identity: the name, logo, colour palette, messaging and overall reputation of the business. Your personal brand, on the other hand, is you: your voice, your values, your story and your unique approach to estate agency.

In the high-value market, it's often your personal brand that initially opens the door, and this is then supported by your business brand, which reinforces the message. It's why you will often see clients following great estate agents when they move to a different brand. Those clients are bought into the agent, not the business.

This is especially relevant for independent agents or boutique agencies. Your personal brand often becomes the business brand in the early stages, and this gives you a massive advantage over seemingly faceless and impersonal corporate brands, however well-known they may be. Remember that, especially when it comes to a home, your clients are not just buying a service; they are buying into *you*.

You Already Have a Brand, Whether You've Built It Intentionally or Not

Here's the truth: Everyone already has a personal brand. Whether or not you've deliberately crafted it or whether you've even realised it, people are forming perceptions about you based on your online presence, your conversations, how you present yourself and how you do business.

The question is not, "Do you have a brand?" It's "What is your brand saying about you?"

Your power comes when you start becoming intentional about shaping that perception, rather than leaving it to chance.

The Core Elements of a Powerful Personal Brand

Here are the key elements that should form the foundation of your personal brand:

Your identity is who you are, what you stand for and how you want to be known. This includes your values, personality and positioning.

Your message is what you believe, how you help and why you do what you do. This becomes the narrative that you share through your marketing and conversations.

Your presence is how you show up, both online and offline. This includes your social media, video content, tone of voice and visual style.

Your proof or your results include testimonials from happy clients, success stories and track record. This helps build trust and credibility.

Your audience or who you're speaking to and who you're trying to attract. A personal brand without a clear target audience is just noise.

When you build these elements with intention and consistency, you become magnetic to the right clients and repelling to the wrong ones. We're not talking about being someone you're not here. Authenticity is key. It's about understanding your personal brand and playing to your strengths.

Personal Branding in Estate Agency

When it comes to selling high-value homes, we're sorry to say that skill alone isn't enough. If you've ever seen another agent – who you know isn't as skilled as you are – land the listing for a home you really wanted, you'll know exactly what we mean (and this has happened to us more than once!).

It's frustrating but true. You could be the most experienced negotiator, the most accurate valuer or the hardest working agent you know, but if no one knows who you are, what you stand for or what makes you different, you'll continually find yourself being overlooked, undercut or undervalued.

In this market, people don't just choose the best agent; they choose the one they perceive to be the best. And that perception is built through your personal brand.

People Buy People

Luxury home sellers are entrusting you with a significant asset, and they want someone who feels like a safe, credible and confident choice. You simply can't get that feeling from a generic company logo or leaflet. It stems from a personal connection, a sense that you are the expert, the advisor and the trusted authority.

Your knowledge, confidence, network, negotiation skills and ability to remain calm under pressure are all things that high-value clients are really looking for. So, if you are the product, then think of your personal brand as the packaging, positioning and promise.

By building your personal brand, you're allowing your potential clients to get to know, like and trust you before they even pick up the phone. And when you do it well, it becomes the reason someone chooses you over every other option in the market – and loyalty sticks with you when things get tricky.

High-net-worth clients are used to dealing with personal brands. It's likely that their lawyer, financial adviser and interior designer will all have been chosen based on reputation, personal connection, and perceived status.

They don't pick from a price list; they pick from those they trust, who they consider experts and who reflect their own aspirations or values. That's why we'd encourage you to see personal branding as a non-negotiable, not just a "nice to have."

Real-World Examples: Personal Brands That Dominate the Industry

Let's look at some international real-estate agents who've turned their personal brands into global empires. These are some of the agents we most admire:

Ryan Serhant (New York)

A former actor turned real-estate powerhouse, Ryan is now one of the most recognised agents in the world (and one of our favourite agents to follow on social media). If you haven't read his books, *Sell it Like Serhant* and *Big Money Energy*, then go out and buy them today! Ryan didn't just build a business; he built a media machine. Through reality TV shows such as *Million Dollar Listing*, social media, YouTube, books and speaking engagements, Ryan has crafted a personal brand that exudes luxury, confidence and hustle.

His personal brand didn't just elevate him; it elevated the visibility and value of every property he listed. Clients want to be associated with his brand – now that's influence!

Josh Altman (Los Angeles)

Josh Altman, another reality star, built his personal brand around being a relentless dealmaker in the celebrity-driven, ultra-luxury Los Angeles market. His confidence, straight-talking style and visible results have made him the go-to agent for high-net-worth clients who want someone who will get the job done. Most recently, Josh has teamed up with his wife and business partner, Heather, and together they have built a formidable brand as a powerhouse couple.

Dolly Lenz (New York)

She might not be a household name, but Dolly has sold billions in real estate and, unlike some of the more flashy media names, her brand is all about discretion, expertise and ultra-high-end service. Dolly has built her brand on credibility and results and she's proof that your personal brand doesn't need to be loud – it just needs to be clear and consistent.

Personal Branding Beyond Property: Lessons From Business Icons

It's not just estate agents who've mastered personal branding. Some of the world's most successful entrepreneurs and business leaders have leveraged their personal brands to build global empires.

Elon Musk (Tesla, SpaceX)

Elon's personal brand is inseparable from his companies. His boldness, innovation and unfiltered presence on social media make him a magnet for attention, talent and investment. Love him or hate him, Elon is proof that a strong personal brand can outshine even the company itself.

Oprah Winfrey (OWN, Harpo)

Oprah built a multi-billion-dollar business on the foundation of her personal brand: authenticity, trust and empowerment. Her name alone carries weight and credibility across many industries. She didn't just build a company; she built a movement.

Richard Branson (Virgin Group)

Branson's adventurous, rebellious spirit has become synonymous with the Virgin brand. He *is* the brand, and that personal touch is what keeps the public engaged and loyal, even across dozens of unrelated industries.

The Lesson for You as a High-Value Agent

Now, we're not suggesting that you need to become the next Elon Musk to gain visibility, but when you operate at the upper end of the market, remember that *you're* the brand. Not your agency, not your marketing materials. You.

Your personal brand becomes the shortcut to trust. It gives people a reason to believe you can deliver results, handle complex negotiations, protect their assets and represent their homes effectively.

You can't hide at the higher end. If you want to break into the high-value home market or grow within it, you need to be seen. You need to be known. And you need to give people a reason to trust you with their home. It's not about being "famous" or well-known for the sake of it. It's about being known for something valuable by the right people.

Using Your Personal Brand to Win More Instructions and Command Higher Fees

The market is saturated with agents. From national chains to boutique independents, online platforms to one-man bands, sellers today have more choices than ever. And for the avoidance of doubt, we believe that's a good thing. It's important that sellers have a choice; a bit of healthy competition keeps standards high and keeps us agents on our toes.

So why should anyone choose you? And more importantly, why should they choose you and pay you more?

The answer lies in your personal brand. Because when you have a clear, compelling and credible personal brand, you no longer compete on price – you compete on perception, value and trust.

When your brand is strong, the fee becomes a secondary conversation. A well-positioned personal brand puts you in a category of one. You're no longer compared to the agent who charges 1% and drops their fee at the first objection. You're the expert professional who has a visible reputation, shows up with value, delivers results that others talk about and speaks with clarity, confidence and authority. That's worth paying more for.

How Your Brand Wins You Instructions

Let's walk through the practical ways that your personal brand gives you the edge at the instruction stage:

You're Already Known Before the Appointment

A strong personal brand means the client has already seen your face, read your posts, watched your videos and heard about your results long before you've stepped through the door. All the heavy lifting has been done for you, and by the time you walk into the listing appointment, you're doing so with pre-built trust. It's a great feeling when we walk into a listing appointment, and the client says, "I feel like I already know you because you seem to be everywhere."

You Frame the Conversation

Your personal brand allows you to be in control. You're not reacting to your client's questions; you're leading the conversation. This can mean that you're not drawn into conversations justifying your fee. Instead, you're demonstrating the value behind it. You shift from "Why do you charge more than the agent down the road?" to "Here's what we do differently that gets our clients superior results."

You Have Social Proof to Support Your Claims

When your brand features visible testimonials, success stories and recognition, prospects see you as someone others have trusted. They feel safer choosing you – even if your fee is higher – because they see the track record.

You're Not Seen as a Commodity

Agents who look and sound the same get compared on one thing: price. But when your personal brand showcases your unique process, thinking, strategy and results, you're no longer just "an agent" – you're a specialist. And specialists get paid more. Just like private doctors, architects or solicitors, clients expect to pay a premium for someone who clearly knows what they're doing.

You Create Perceived Value Before You Even Meet

Your content, reputation and message build up the value perception long before the fee conversation ever happens. So, when you say your fee is 2%, the client doesn't flinch. Because you've already shown why you're worth it. Remember that value isn't just about what you do; it's about how clearly you communicate it.

You Stand for Something

Strong brands stand for something. And that makes you more attractive to the right clients means the wrong ones opt out on their own. When your values are clear, such as "no cutting corners," "high-touch, not high volume," or "discreet, boutique service," you naturally attract sellers who share those values. And those sellers are far less likely to haggle over your fee.

How to Craft Your Personal Brand Message

You've probably heard the phrase, "Your vibe attracts your tribe." In estate agency, this couldn't be more true. The way you speak, show up and communicate your message determines who you attract, how much they trust you and whether they see you as "just another estate agent" or the expert they want to work with.

Your personal brand message is the clear, consistent narrative that tells people who you help, what you do, what makes you different and why it matters (to them).

It's not a sales pitch, it's a positioning statement. It helps people "get you" in seconds. And when it's crafted with skill and intention, it becomes the anchor for all your marketing, networking, content and conversations.

So, how should you go about creating your own? Let's walk you through it step by step:

Bringing It All Together: Crafting Your Personal Brand Message

In Chapter 3, we guided you through the process of creating and defining your Vision, Mission and Values. Now, you have the raw materials for one of the most powerful tools in your business: your personal brand message. This is the clear, compelling story you tell the world about who you are, what you do and why it matters. It's the essence of your reputation, and it's what helps high-value homeowners feel connected to you and not just your service.

Here's how to turn your Vision, Mission and Values into a personal brand message:

Know Your Niche

Before you can craft a compelling message, you need to know exactly who you're talking to. Remember that high-value clients are looking for a specialist, not a generalist. They want someone who truly understands their world, their priorities and their lifestyle. Where do you specialise? Is it luxury penthouses in the city? Country estates for families outside London? High-end homes in a specific postcode or gated community? Architecturally unique or design-led homes? Properties for overseas buyers relocating to the UK?

The clearer you are about your niche, the more resonant your message becomes. When someone feels you are talking directly to them, they're far more likely to trust you.

Lead With Your Why (Mission)

Your mission is your heartbeat. It shows clients that you're not in this for the quick win. You're here to make a meaningful impact. Start your brand message with this deeper purpose.

Think: *I help owners of unique and beautiful homes sell with confidence, clarity and maximum impact because I believe everyone deserves a better experience than the traditional estate agent offers.*

This isn't about puffery; it's about passion. Why do you do what you do? Lead with that.

Anchor in Your Values

Your values shape the way you work, and when you communicate them clearly, you attract clients who share your ethos. This is especially important at the high end of the market, where trust, discretion and shared values often matter more than price.

For example:

"Known for integrity, creativity and exacting standards, I'm proud to offer a service that reflects what I'd expect for my own home."

Don't be afraid to show what you *stand for*. It's how people decide if they're aligned with you.

Point to the Bigger Picture (Vision)

Your vision gives clients confidence that you're not just reactive; you're intentional, ambitious and here for the long game. Whether it's raising industry standards or becoming the go-to agent in your area, sharing your vision builds buy-in.

Example:

> "My goal is to set a new benchmark for selling high-value homes in Oxfordshire, combining world-class marketing with a deeply personal approach."

It shows leadership. Clients want to work with someone who's not just part of the market, but shaping it.

Wrap It Up in a Human, Memorable Way

Now tie it all together into a brand message that you can use on your website, in your social media bios and in your listing presentations. Aim for a few punchy sentences that blend your mission, values and vision into a confident, cohesive message.

Here's a simple structure:

> "I help [ideal client] achieve [specific outcome] by delivering [unique service or approach]. I believe [core belief], and I'm on a mission to [mission]. My goal is to [vision]."

Example:

> "I help discerning homeowners sell unique and high-value homes for the best possible price, with less stress and more confidence. I believe estate agencies should be personal, not pushy, and I'm on a mission to raise the bar for what sellers should expect. My goal? To become the most trusted name in premium property sales in Oxfordshire."

"I help busy professionals sell architecturally unique homes in London by combining high-impact marketing with strategic negotiation, so they get maximum value with minimum hassle."

"I work with the owners of unique homes in Buckinghamshire who want a more intelligent, boutique-style selling experience that's focused on results, discretion and expert advice."

This becomes the spine of your brand. It drives your tone of voice, your visuals and the experience clients have at every touchpoint. Remember that your message should be clear and simple so that someone can understand exactly what you do within a couple of sentences.

Becoming Known: Using Your Personal Brand to Increase Visibility

Now you've clarified your niche, defined your values and crafted your personal message. It's time for the next crucial step: getting seen.

Because no matter how great your service is, or how beautifully written your marketing message is, if no one knows about you, none of it matters.

Your visibility will make the difference between you being good and you being in demand. In the high-value property market, clients don't just stumble across you by accident. You must create a presence that gets you noticed, builds trust and keeps you top of mind with the right people.

In today's world, perception is reality. It's why the agent who appears to be the expert often wins the instruction, even though they may not be the most experienced or the best. It's because people trust what they can see. When you increase your visibility, you build trust through familiarity, gain authority by showing up consistently, create more opportunities through referrals, media and partnerships and attract high-quality clients who already feel like they know you.

So how do you do it? As always, we've told you the "why," and now we won't leave you without telling you the "how."

Here's our framework to help you increase visibility and establish yourself as *the* go-to expert in your market. It's the framework we've used to successfully build our luxury brand, Stowhill Estates, and it's what we teach our partner agents who are establishing themselves in new areas.

Own Your Digital Presence

High-value homeowners will almost certainly Google you before they meet you, or even before they pick up the phone to book that first meeting. What they see online about you will either build their trust and confidence in you or break it.

So, make sure your social media pages are optimised and look professional. If your Facebook profile is set to public, you might want to consider removing the drunken Ibiza holiday photos. Some rules of thumb are:

- Use a high-quality, professional photo, particularly on LinkedIn
- Write a compelling bio that speaks to your niche and values (Pro-tip: Use ChatGPT to help you craft this)
- Share consistent content that positions you as an expert
- Stay away from sharing any extreme political or personal views – keep it light, but keep it professional

Remember that high-value clients look for subtle signs of professionalism, so your tone of voice, grammar, language and attention to detail all count.

Create Thoughtful, Value-Driven Content

If visibility is the goal, content is the vehicle. You need to demonstrate what you know, rather than just stating it. Start creating and sharing content that demonstrates your expertise and provides value to the reader. You don't need to start dancing on TikTok, but you do need to be visible to add value. Some content ideas might be:

- Insights into the high-value homes market in your area
- Behind-the-scenes footage of how you get ready to market a unique home
- Short educational videos (e.g. "3 Common Mistakes to Avoid When Selling Your High-Value Home")
- Case studies or success stories

- Personal stories that reflect your values and journey

- Thought leadership posts on LinkedIn or blog articles

Use Video to Build Instant Connection

Video is a game-changer for personal branding. It allows people to get to know you, to see your face, hear your voice and feel your energy before they've even met you in person.

You don't need a film crew or a fancy camera. Just use your phone and be authentic and insightful. Just be you! Some ideas you might want to try:

- Property walk-through with a commentary

- Weekly "market minute" updates

- Client Q&A's or myth-busting

- Personal stories that show your passion and personality

It's perfectly normal to feel awkward at first – we all do! But keep going, and we promise that it will feel natural after just a few times. (Pro-tip: It's easier to go live on a Facebook or Instagram video and be authentically you than it is to try and pre-record the "perfect" video 40 times.)

Show Up in the Right Circles

Remember that visibility isn't just digital, so you can't expect to gain recognition by hiding behind your computer screen. High-value clients often move in tight-knit circles, so be intentional about establishing a presence in the right local or professional networks.

You could try:

- Attending premium lifestyle or business networking events
- Hosting a small educational workshop for local homeowners
- Partnering with interior designers, architects, solicitors or wealth managers
- Contributing to local publications or podcasts

People refer to those they remember. So stay visible, stay valuable and stay top of mind!

Be Consistent, Not Constant

If all this sounds overwhelming, remember that you don't need to be everywhere; you just need to be somewhere consistently. Pick 1-2 platforms that suit your audience and your style (e.g. Instagram for visual storytelling, LinkedIn for thought leadership) and commit to showing up regularly. A simple weekly system will ensure that you show up consistently in the right places. It might include:

- 1 video or educational post
- 1 behind-the-scenes or lifestyle post
- 1 personal or values-based post
- 1 engagement session (replying to DMs, commenting on other people's content)

Bonus: Use Local or National Media to Amplify Your Message

As your personal brand grows, consider exploring opportunities to get featured in local or national press. Trust us when we say you shouldn't wait to get discovered; you need to put yourself out there. Position yourself as an expert by pitching stories or providing insight to journalists. You could try:

- Writing an opinion piece about your local market
- Sharing unique property stories with lifestyle publications
- Offering tips to homeowners in the national press or radio
- Applying for industry awards

Using Storytelling to Build Your Personal Brand

Facts tell. Stories Sell.

Storytelling is one of the most powerful tools in your brand-building arsenal because people don't connect to data; they connect to emotion. When you're creating your content, think about how you could turn each piece into a story. Some types of stories might include:

Client Journeys

Tell the story of a real client (with permission, of course) and walk people through the challenge they faced, how you helped, and the outcome you created.

"When Sarah called me, she had already had her house listed with two different agents for six months. Nothing. Within 14 days of working with me, we had three viewings, two offers and a sale at £75,000 over the previous valuation."

Stories like these create instant trust because they show proof of your process in action.

Behind-the-Scenes Insights

Show people how you think and work. Bring them into your world.

"Here's what most agents get wrong when marketing a £1m home…"

"Why we used a private off-market strategy for this particular seller…"

Personal Stories

Don't be afraid to share glimpses of your journey, values or lessons learned.

"I remember the first time I stepped into a £2m home. I felt intimidated. Now I coach other agents on how to walk in with confidence."

These stories make you human, relatable and memorable. The most powerful stories are rooted in emotion, not ego. Focus on the client's journey and the value you added.

Social Proof: Let Others Do the Talking

It's one thing for you to say you're great. It's another thing entirely when someone else does it for you. Social proof builds trust faster than almost anything else, especially in the high-value homes market.

You can use testimonials and case studies from past clients discussing their experiences working with you – what stood out, what was different and what the outcome was. Don't be afraid to go a bit deeper: share full breakdowns of challenging sales, impressive outcomes or strategic marketing approaches. Include before-and-after photos, numbers and timelines.

Using Your Personal Brand to Get Referrals and Recommendations

Imagine a business where your phone rings with warm leads. Where clients say, "I was told that I have to speak to you..." Where your best instructions come not just from cold calls, but from referrals.

This isn't luck. It's leverage.

And the key to unlocking it is your brand reputation.

Because in the high-value homes market, who you are matters just as much as what you do. And when you become known as the agent who delivers an exceptional experience with integrity, results and elegance, people talk.

In a world full of noise, ads and empty promises, a personal referral cuts through it all. Referrals come with pre-built trust, less price resistance, higher conversion rates, aligned values and expectations and lower marketing spend. Your prospects have already been pre-sold on you!

But to build a referral-based business, you must first become a referrable brand. Ask yourself:

"Would I refer me?"

"Am I consistently remarkable in the way I show up and deliver?"

"Do I create moments that clients want to talk about?"

"Does my brand feel personal, consistent and memorable?"

Make yourself memorable by being remarkable. You don't want past clients to say, "Yeah, they were nice." You want them to say, "You must speak to them. They were incredible!"

That sort of referral comes from branding that is clear, consistent, distinctive and emotionally resonant. People refer people who leave an impression, not just provide a service.

One of the smartest moves you can make is to systemise your referrals by building referral opportunities throughout the customer journey. This could include thank-you cards or gifts, email sequences, client satisfaction surveys and anniversary check-ins.

Remember that referrals don't happen by luck; they happen by design. So, if you want more referrals, be unforgettable, serve as if it matters (because it does), stay visible and valuable and build a brand that people like and trust enough to share.

Mindset Shift: Visibility Is a Form of Service

You may be feeling some resistance to becoming more visible at this point. And we get it; you're not alone. Many agents we have coached or worked with have hesitated to put themselves out there because they fear it feels "sales-y" or "self-promotional." But here's the mindset shift you'll need to adopt: Visibility is a service if you're offering real value, insight or inspiration to others.

Each story you share, each piece of content you post, and each success you highlight all stack up to form the perception of you in your market. And over time, that perception becomes your reputation. You become the agent people recognise, you become the agent they refer to and you become the agent they can trust.

When you increase your visibility as a high-value agent, you're not just marketing. You're helping people make better decisions, feel more confident and have more trust in you before they even pick up the phone. In fact, you are doing a disservice to those people who really need you by not putting yourself out there. So, don't make yourself the best-kept secret in your industry. Don't let your prospect choose an inferior agent because they don't know about you – that's doing them a massive disservice! Start showing up today, and let your presence be your power!

Stop Pitching, Start Positioning

When you lean into your personal brand, you stop convincing and start attracting. You show up already trusted, already respected and already valuable. When that happens, everything shifts. You get to hear "yes" more often, you're asked to discount less, your ideal clients start referring you to their friends and you get more ideal clients. Building your personal brand doesn't just get you more business; it helps you build the kind of business you actually want.

Your personal brand isn't a logo, a colour palette or a perfectly curated Instagram grid. It's the feeling people get when they see your name. It's the reputation that precedes you. It's the value you represent in the minds and hearts of your ideal clients.

In the high-value homes market, where trust is everything and service expectations are sky-high, your personal brand can become your most powerful tool. It helps you stand out in a crowded market and attract high-quality clients who align with your values. It helps you command premium fees without resistance. It helps you win instructions based on perception and trust, not just price. And most importantly, it helps create long-term loyalty, referrals and industry recognition.

But none of this happens by accident. It's built intentionally. Your personal brand is something you must craft with care. It's not about being famous; it's about being known, respected and remembered by the right people, for all the right reasons. Start where you are and be consistent. Your personal brand is a living, evolving asset that grows with you. The more intention, clarity and heart you bring to it, the more powerful it becomes.

You don't need to be the loudest, flashiest or most followed agent. You just need to be the one that your clients trust. Let your brand do the heavy lifting, and your reputation open the doors, while you build a business that not only performs but feels authentic to you.

We've created a free worksheet to help you craft your Personal Brand Message. Visit www.eliteagentcollective.com/resources to download it or scan the QR code located on the back of the book.

Chapter 5
Your Ideal Client Is Looking for You!

Discovering Clients Who Bring You Joy and Fulfilment in Your Work and Avoiding the "Conveyor Belt Of Arseholes"

Let's start with a radical idea: You are not supposed to work with everyone.

When you're new in business, it's easy to fall into the trap of saying "yes" to every opportunity, every valuation, every slightly interested homeowner. You take on every instruction, grit your teeth through difficult clients and convince yourself that "it's just part of the job."

But what if it isn't?

What if the single biggest shift you could make in your business (and your sanity) is to stop chasing everyone and start intentionally attracting just the right people? The ones who light you up, respect your process, value your time and happily pay your fee without question?

This chapter is about helping you define who those people are.

Because, as we've said before, who you say "no" to is as important as who you say "yes" to. We'll walk you through why working with the wrong clients can tank your energy, your profitability and your passion, and how to build a business full of clients who energise and inspire you. We'll show you how to create a clear, detailed "Ideal Client Avatar" and how this one exercise can transform your marketing, your messaging and your mindset.

Because when you know exactly who you're here to serve, everything gets easier. Conversations flow. Fees feel natural. Referrals multiply. And you stop trying to prove your worth because your clients already see it.

What Do We Actually Mean by "Ideal Client"?

Your Ideal Client is the kind of person you genuinely love working with, the one who "gets" you, respects your time, trusts your advice, pays your fee without flinching and makes the whole process feel less like hard work and more like a collaboration. They're the people who energise you, not drain you. They value what you offer, they refer you to their friends and they make you proud of the business you've built. We've all had clients like this, and they're a joy to work with and can make all your effort feel so worthwhile.

Importantly, your Ideal Client isn't just about budget or postcode. It's about aligning values, communication style and mutual respect. It's the client who feels like they're a great fit from the very first conversation. That's who we're talking about here. And the more of them you can attract, the more joyful, profitable and sustainable your business becomes.

Why This Work Will Change Everything

If you only take one thing away from this book, understanding the philosophy behind working with your Ideal Client will be game-changing for you. Trust us. This stuff is important.

When you take the time to get crystal clear on who your Ideal Client is and you build your business around attracting only those people, everything changes. Your conversations flow more naturally. Your fees are easier to quote (and receive). Your marketing starts to land with the right people. You stop second-guessing yourself and you start enjoying your work again.

And beyond the business wins? You get your evenings back. Your weekends. Your energy. Your self-belief. You take pride in what you've built. Because when you choose to work only with clients who align with your values, appreciate your expertise and genuinely want what you uniquely offer, your business becomes more profitable, more fulfilling and more sustainable.

This isn't just about who you serve; it's about how you feel while serving them.

None of us went into business to work with a "conveyor belt of arseholes" – Michael's favourite expression! Chances are that, like us, you started your business to have freedom and choice to work with people you actually like, not people you have to be nice to just because your boss told you to. But how many of us have ended up working with toxic clients because we needed the money, only to find ourselves down the line dejected, depleted and poorer as a result of taking on too many of the wrong clients?

Are Your Clients Radiators or Drains?

Take a moment to pause and ask yourself, "Do I really know who my Ideal Client is?" Not just in theory, but in real, tangible detail. Who have you been working with up to now? When you look back over your last five or ten clients, how many of them genuinely energised you? How many felt aligned, easy to work with and made you feel valued? And how many were, if you're honest, a bit of a nightmare?

The truth is, your current client list is a mirror. It shows you exactly who your marketing and mindset have been attracting. So ask yourself: Are you surrounded by radiators or drains? Are you working with people who energise you and move your business forward, or with those who exhaust you, question your worth and chip away at your confidence?

If you are already in business and haven't done the work to discover your Ideal Client avatar, then we're willing to bet that you probably have more than your fair share of difficult and/or demanding clients to deal with. These are the "Drains": Clients who make unreasonable demands on your time, clients who question your fee, or your methods – or both.

By contrast, clients who are "Radiators" leave you feeling excited to go to work, pay you well and on time and value your time and your work. Working with these people is a relationship built on trust and not a transaction. They're loyal to you and become raving fans who give you repeat business and refer you to their friends. Clients like these make being in business a joy and leave you feeling deeply fulfilled and handsomely rewarded.

How to Spot Who's NOT Your Ideal Client

Sometimes, the easiest way to define your Ideal Client is to first get clear on who definitely isn't. These are the people who make your stomach drop when their name flashes up on your phone. The ones who second-guess your advice, haggle on your fee, drain your energy, ignore your boundaries and make you question why you started this business in the first place.

If you find yourself justifying their behaviour, overriding your gut or thinking, "I can fix this one," that's a sign. Your non-Ideal Clients often come with red flags right from the start: They don't respect your process, they treat your expertise like a commodity and working with them feels hard from day one. Listen to that discomfort. It's your business's way of telling you to walk away. Because every time you say yes to a non-Ideal Client, you're saying no to the kind of client you *really* want to work with.

Now, let's be realistic for a second; this is an imperfect science. Sometimes, you just have to go through a bit of trial and error before you start to recognise the types of people you love working with and the types you'd rather lovingly say "no" to.

We know you won't get it right every time, and you might need to work with a few bad apples, so that you know who you definitely don't want to work with. You'll get it right or you'll learn, and both outcomes are fine. This is an ongoing and organic process. Practice it and you'll improve over time. You'll learn to spot the terrible client and the perfect client earlier in the process as you become more skilled in recognition, saving you time, money and heartache.

Your Ideal Client May Evolve Over Time

Our Ideal Client has definitely changed over the last decade. To give you an idea, when we were first starting out, our Ideal Clients were Geoff and Yvonne. Mid-70s with a large house that they'd lived in for 25 to 30 years. They were "accidental millionaires," which means they had purchased their family home in the late 80s or early 90s for a sum that seems ridiculously small now, and the house value had soared during the time they lived there. They were looking to downsize to release equity for their retirement or to give to their children or grandchildren, and appreciated old-fashioned values such as white-glove service, a phone call rather than an email and doing business on a handshake. You'd be likely to find Geoff at the golf club and Yvonne at a Women's Institute meeting.

We still enjoy working with individuals who share these values, and their perspectives align closely with our own. But these days, our Ideal Client skews a little younger. They will probably be in their late 40s to mid-50s, entrepreneurial, risk-takers who want to work with a disruptive business, not a dusty old corporate dinosaur. They understand modern marketing mediums like YouTube, Instagram and TikTok and tend to own a spectacular home decorated with the latest interior design trends. They really "get" what we do, and so our listing appointments with these types feel easy and natural. There's no hard sell, and they are happy to pay our fee because they recognise our worth.

A conversation with these types feels more like a chat with friends than a sales pitch. There are no "scripts" to memorise, no sales pattern. We just listen, engage and provide solutions. They've seen our marketing and are attracted to the way we do business. This means that the hard work of landing the client is 90% done before we've even walked through the door. They become raving fans and refer us to their friends. We don't have to explain or justify our product or service or "sell" ourselves to them.

We simply love doing business with this type of person and are excited to showcase their beautiful homes, delivering results that will blow them away. Sounds wonderful, doesn't it? And it really is. All because we have taken the time to discover and document who our Ideal Client is, and have created marketing that is specifically designed to appeal to that person. It creates a beautiful synergy when you become an "attraction marketer."

And you can do this, too. It's very simple, but it requires a bit of focus and the ability to be truly honest with yourself about the kind of people you like and dislike working with, and then sticking to your convictions.

Why Does It Matter? Can't I Just Work With Anyone?

Think about some of the world's biggest and most successful brands. We guarantee that the brands you love most have created their marketing messaging with you in mind. There's a well-known saying in marketing that if you try to speak to everyone, you end up speaking to no one.

Every great business solves a specific problem for a specific person. These businesses understand the aspirations, fears and motivations of their Ideal Clients and then solve a problem for them. Tony Robbins says that the key to growing your business is to understand your clients' greatest pain points and desires. Of course, you can argue that there are millions of people who own a house and who could become house-selling clients. It's easy to believe that every homeowner has the potential to work with you, and therefore, you should try and cast your marketing net as wide as possible. We really hope to dispel that myth in the following chapter and convince you to niche your offering down to a select group of hand-picked clients.

For a long time, it seemed as though the only types of people we were attracting into our business were the arseholes. We'd grit our teeth and get through the deal (whilst drinking away the pain and frustration), only to find that as soon as we got rid of one toxic client, another came along to fill their place – a bit like the conveyor belt on *The Generation Game*. Only this time, there weren't any prizes; just horrible, toxic clients who brought with them more struggles, sleepless nights and left us questioning why on earth we ever started this business.

If you're feeling stuck working with clients who are less than ideal, we encourage you to believe that there's a world where you work *only* with your Ideal Client – The Radiators! These are the ones who bring you fulfilment and joy, who pay you what you're worth and who make going to work a pleasure. But it requires a fundamental mindset shift.

This was a huge learning experience for us both, and we went through a lot of challenging and stressful times before we truly understood that we could work with clients who love what we do, value our input and professionalism, respect our time and boundaries and will happily pay us what we're worth.

But before we fully embraced that truth? We paid the price – over and over again.

Let us tell you about one client we'll never forget.

The One Client We'll Never Forget (as told by Michael)

We were instructed on a £3m property – our highest-value listing to date – and at first, the size of the potential commission cheque completely overshadowed the quiet alarm bells going off in the background.

The house itself wasn't exactly a showstopper inside – think fake Greek columns (with strict instructions of "no touching"), lilac ceilings, dark wood wardrobes and enough marble to build a small palace. There were more fake Greek touches than you could shake a toga at. But the grounds? Absolutely stunning. A private pub, a triple garage, a separate cottage and a blossom-lined garden that genuinely looked like something out of a dream.

The sellers were a couple, and the woman was lovely. The man was... less so. We should never have taken the instruction, but we were still relatively new, eager and chasing big deals. Against our better judgment, we said yes.

From the get-go, the red flags were flapping wildly. His first instruction to us was delivered in a tone that suggested it wasn't up for negotiation: "NO ONE CAN TAKE ANY PHOTOS DURING A VIEWING, AND IF I SEE THEM DOING SO, THEY CAN FUCK OFF!" We politely pointed out that the house was already plastered all over the internet, but he remained utterly unmoved. Still, we pressed on. Big fee, big prize. What could possibly go wrong?

Answer: Everything.

Weeks passed without a single offer. Hardly surprising, considering one potential buyer didn't even bother getting out of the car before declaring, "Not for us!" Eventually, we recommended a price reduction. His response? He fired us. Via a gloriously blunt email.

However, the very next day, his wife called us, full of apologies and asked if we would continue marketing the property at the reduced price. Against all reason (and demonstrating a stunning lack of self-preservation instincts), we agreed.

Finally, a young Asian lady arrived for a viewing, along with her entourage. She barely spent ten minutes inside, and we thought it was another write-off – until she stepped into the blossom-filled garden. Her face lit up. She instinctively pulled out her phone and snapped a picture.

Before I could even blink, the seller came storming out of his greenhouse (where he was potting, no joke, about 7,000 plants) like a man possessed, bellowing: "SHE'S TAKEN A FUCKING PHOTOGRAPH! EITHER SHE STOPS, OR SHE CAN FUCK OFF!"

We managed to calm things down, but it was yet another painful reminder that this man was an absolute powder keg.

The next day, her assistant called and submitted an all-cash offer of £2.7 million. Delighted, I rang the seller, expecting a celebration. Instead, I was met with: "IF YOU'RE CALLING

WITH AN OFFER FROM THAT BITCH, SHE CAN FUCK OFF!"

Click.

Stunned, I called back – because legally, I had to submit the offer – and was hung up on again, with a few extra insults thrown in for good measure.

Miraculously, the buyer upped her offer to the full asking price of £2.75 million. Another phone call. This time, after a tirade that included several racially charged comments (unbelievable in this day and age), he reluctantly accepted on the strict condition that the exchange had to happen within four weeks or the deal was off.

Against all odds, we managed to pull it off. Four weeks later, contracts were exchanged. We celebrated (quietly — we weren't counting our chickens yet).

And then COVID-19 hit.

The buyers' solicitor requested a short delay in completion due to lockdown logistics. The seller's response?

An emphatic "no."

Completion day came and went. The buyers were technically in breach, but they had ten days to rectify the situation. Meanwhile, the seller rang us daily to shout, threaten lawsuits and remind me in no uncertain terms that if I thought I'd be getting paid, we could "have that pissing contest later."

Days passed. Silence. No news from the solicitor. No news from the seller. We braced ourselves for a full-on legal nightmare.

And then, unbelievably, it turned out they had completed it *on time*. They just "forgot" to tell us.

I had to chase the solicitors repeatedly to get our fee, and when it eventually arrived, it felt hollow. We weren't celebrating. We were exhausted and emotionally wrung out. No amount of money could have made up for the sheer misery of that transaction.

Later, we heard through the grapevine (specifically from the poor estate agent selling him his next home) that he'd been just as charming with her. Apparently, he told her to "fuck off" multiple times, too. No surprises there.

When the dust finally settled, we spoke to our business coach. We explained, over a large glass of wine, that although the fee had been good, the toll it had taken on our mental health, relationships and happiness was far too high. Her advice?

"Write him a letter. Say absolutely everything you want to say. Then burn it. And open a really expensive bottle of champagne."

We did. It was one of the most cathartic things we've ever done. Highly recommend it.

That whole experience taught us something priceless: Never ignore the red flags. Never let the promise of a big fee cloud your judgment. Never work with clients who make you feel sick to your stomach.

Because no amount of money is worth selling your sanity.

It's an extreme example, yes, but that's exactly why it matters. Because when you work with the wrong clients, it's not just frustrating – it can be deeply damaging. To your confidence, energy, team culture and bank balance. This experience taught us, loud and clear, that no potential fee is worth the emotional fallout of a toxic relationship. When you compromise on fit, you compromise on everything. And the real tragedy? That time and energy could have been spent serving clients who love what you do, value your voice and make this business the joy it's meant to be.

We Know Saying "No" Is Scary!

We totally get it: When you're just starting out with no money and no instructions, you look everywhere for an opportunity. It can feel scary to be discerning about the types of people you want to work with, as you fear missing out on opportunities. We know just how difficult it can be when your bank account is at zero and that seller agrees to market their house with you as long as you can "discount your fee."

We've done it so many times. Enough times to say we know this for sure: 20% of your most difficult clients will take up 80%

of your time, 80% of your energy and cause 80% of your stress. What's more, dealing with this seemingly small but highly disruptive 20% will prevent you from focusing on the clients who really need you, really value you and can be your greatest supporters and champions.

We have worked with so many difficult, demanding and sometimes toxic clients that at times we honestly both felt like throwing in the towel. It created a false belief in us both that wealthy people with large houses to sell were inherently difficult to work with. It turns out that we were attracting this with *our* toxic mindsets, so we did a lot of work on fixing those negative belief patterns.

It wasn't until our friends pointed out during our regular mastermind meetings that we always seemed to attract incredible clients—and always had a dramatic story to tell— that we began to question things. What were we doing (or not doing) that kept landing us in the same situation every time: stressed, demoralised and poor? One of our closest industry friends (and all-around amazing agent), Sara-May Smith, said to us one day, "You two always seem to work with the *worst* people! Where on earth do you find them?"

It was a lightbulb moment. Some of our clients had left us scared, demoralised, angry, snappy with our children, unable to sleep, unable to relax and enjoy downtime and as a result, we were physically ill. We had both gained over four stone in two years and were looking and feeling terrible. Something had to change – and that something was us.

While we don't want to dwell too much on the past now that we are 100% focused on looking forward and working only with clients who bring us fulfilment and joy, it's worth sharing a few more anecdotes in case they are helpful. At the very least, we hope they amuse you, and you'll know we've been there too!

The only good thing to say about some of the toxic clients we've worked with in the past is that our experiences with them make for some good anecdotes at dinner parties and in this book!

We've had Mr A (the A stands for Angry), who was just pissed off at the world all the time. Being natural people pleasers, we both were convinced that we could win him over with our charm and work ethic, as well as wanting to list his £3m house. Sadly, we didn't realise the impossibility of this task. This guy literally hated everyone! Including the poor couple who eventually bought his house – in cash, for the asking price!

Then we have the highly decorated female police officer who told Lucy to "stop being a patronising bitch" when she suggested she might like to take a deep breath and calm down during a highly charged negotiation.

Then there was the divorcing couple who wouldn't speak to each other and instead communicated through us, their agents, having us work as their unpaid (and inexperienced!) marriage counsellors.

Or the homeowner, who considered herself a "marketing expert," who insisted we re-take all the photographs three times and re-write the property description to her exacting standards, before firing us and relisting with a new agent who took the photos on their iPhone.

After his 30-year sales career, Michael particularly enjoyed working with clients who insisted on "role-playing" the conversation with a potential buyer before every viewing, firing out objections to see how well he'd handle them.

And who could forget the seller who lost their £2m house sale over their refusal to include the £5,000 hot tub in their "fixtures and fittings"?!

The list of these challenging clients could probably fill the whole of this book (Michael has always wanted to write a coffee table book called "A Conveyor Belt of Arseholes"!). And in hindsight, there was one thing in common with all of them: Us! The hardest thing to accept is that ultimately, the responsibility for ignoring all the wildly fluttering red flags and the funny feeling in our stomachs lies only with us. All the signs were there, every single time. We were just so convinced that we could be the "superheroes" that we just ignored them. We were wrong.

Now, we understand with absolute clarity that it's better to learn to spot these sorts of people early on in the process. It's much more beneficial to elegantly walk away than to live in the false hope that you'll somehow be able to change them or that they'll magically turn into wonderful people overnight. We hate to break it to you, but it just isn't going to happen, and not even your incredible personality, unmatched work ethic and world-class service will change that.

So do yourself a huge favour and learn when to walk away. Then, do yourself an even bigger favour and take the time to learn all about your perfect client, so you can begin to attract them into your business.

If you're not discerning about choosing the people you want to work with, you run the risk of working with people like the charmers we have enjoyed. Of course, some of your clients will be perfectly nice, but when you follow the strategies in this chapter, you'll create a virtuous circle of Ideal Clients who will attract more Ideal Clients to you and your business. To put it simply, as marketing expert John Jantsch says, "When you properly target your clients, you no longer need to work with jerks." Sounds good to us!

The more you work with Ideal Clients, the more Ideal Clients you'll attract. The reverse is also true: Continue to choose difficult or toxic clients (even accidentally), and you'll attract more of the same, guaranteed.

Spending the time to create a clear picture of the sort of people you really want to work with (and the sort of people you don't want to work with) creates a framework for you and your team to decide who is a good fit for your business, and make your work more enjoyable and fulfilling as a result.

When you discover who your Ideal Client is and begin to attract them through your marketing and messaging, we promise that doing business with them will no longer feel hard. You'll start to experience a natural flow and synergy that makes it joyful to go to work on a Monday morning, and you'll stop getting that sick feeling in your stomach when you see their name pop up on your phone.

It's really worth spending some time creating the avatar for your Ideal Client, and we'll share some exercises with you that have helped us. If you have more than one person running your business, it's interesting and helpful to do the Ideal Client exercise together and then compare. How far aligned or apart are you in your vision of the perfect client?

Bear in mind that this is not a "one-and-done" exercise. Your Ideal Client and the types of people you enjoy working with can change over time, so this is a process we review and update every single year.

Once you create your Ideal Client Avatar, you'll have a clear picture in your mind of this person (or people), and you can start to create your marketing and messaging around them. It's the secret to creating marketing messages that really hit home with people: They feel as though they are really understood because you have spent time thinking about their fears, hopes and dreams and speaking to them in a way that really resonates.

Now, we're not saying that you can *only* work with these types of clients, and we're not saying that you automatically have to say "no" to someone who doesn't exactly fit the mould. But if you end up with a client base that's made up of 80% Ideal Client, we guarantee you'll find your work more fulfilling, less stressful and more lucrative. Sounds good, doesn't it?

Did you know that humans make buying decisions based on 80% emotion and only 20% logic? That's why identifying and appealing to your Ideal Client will transform your business and increase your conversion rate exponentially. Once you discover who your Ideal Client is and create branding and marketing that is irresistibly appealing to them, it eliminates the competition because they feel like *you* are the only person who truly understands them and can deliver what they need. What you charge, therefore, becomes irrelevant, because they want you and only you, and those low-fee agents don't even come close.

You'll start to notice uncanny synergies and coincidences between you and your Ideal Client. You may own the same item of clothing (our clients love Mint Velvet as much as Lucy does!), or you'll spot them down at the golf club (Michael is always up for a round on the 19th!) You'll likely have things in common – your children might attend the same schools, you'll drive similar cars, holiday in the same places and share a taste in decor (our grasp of the Farrow & Ball palette is second to none!).

No one knows our Ideal Client better than we do. I guarantee you could ask either of us any question about our Ideal Client, and we would be able to give you the same answers. We know they drive a Range Rover or a Tesla and will probably have a "fun" car in the garage. They play golf and are a member of one of Oxfordshire's most prestigious clubs. They have Farrow & Ball paint on their walls and hand-built kitchens. They shop at OKA and The White Company, they play Padel and holiday in the South of France. They appreciate quality and value, and are willing to spend money on understated luxury items that are high-quality, such as Miele, Bang & Olufsen, John Lewis or The Cotswold Company.

Creating Your Ideal Client Avatar

Now, it's over to you to define your Ideal Client and create their avatar. This exercise can be really fun, and we've provided you with a free worksheet you can download from the resources section at the back of this book to help you. Don't be afraid to go deep into the details. This is all about getting to know your Ideal Client intimately so you can better understand their hopes, aspirations, fears and pain points and create solutions that are perfectly matched for them.

Let your imagination run wild when creating your Ideal Client avatar. Give them a name and a personality. You want to really understand these people inside and out, and you can never have enough detail about these people's lives, how they think, what sort of things they say and what their future dreams are.

What are their worries? What keeps them awake at night, and how can you solve their biggest challenges? Remember that your Ideal Client will buy what they want, but you will give them what they need, so attempt to understand them and their motivations in clear detail. Only once you have created your Ideal Client avatar should you start creating your marketing messages, ensuring they will really resonate.

If this is your first time doing this exercise, we recommend focusing on one type of client at a time. Once you grow, you might find that your business serves several different types of clients (but they will probably share a lot of core values). Our advice is to start small and focus on getting to know one type of client at a time, committing to a deep understanding of them. This is the key to creating marketing that works effortlessly.

Exercise: Client Avatar Creation

To get the most out of this exercise, it's important to get really good at asking great questions. Carve out enough time to really go deep on this exercise, and don't skip through it or assume you already know who you serve.

The answers you give to the following questions will help you shape your marketing, so get really, really specific. The clearer and more specific you can be, the more magnetic your marketing will be.

Your Ideal Client will become your avatar for all the marketing you create, and you'll write your messaging with that one person in mind. If this specific approach feels uncomfortable, take a deep breath and trust the process. When you speak to one person, you will magically connect with many. And there's an added bonus: Your non-Ideal Clients will begin to "self-select" themselves out of working with you, saving you time and money. Win-win!

It's helpful to review some of your past clients or sales and categorise them accordingly. Who have been your favourite clients to work for? What made working with them so great?

Ask your best past clients if you can conduct an interview with them. Ask them:

Why did they choose you?

What was their biggest challenge before working with you?

What results did they get from working with you?

A useful framework for discovering your Ideal Client is the F.O.R.D. method. It stands for Family, Occupation, Recreation and Dreams.

Using this method can help you uncover how your clients think and feel and understand their motivations so you can build a deeper and more meaningful relationship with them.

Family
Learning about someone's family setup can be useful in gaining a clear picture of their motivations, what's happening in their lives and what their future plans might be. Are they

downsizers looking to retire and release equity? Or are they moving up the ladder, planning to grow their family and on a path towards their "forever home"? The marketing messages you'll create for these two types of people will be vastly different in their content and tone.

Occupation

Do they run their own business? Are they retired? If they're entrepreneurial, chances are they'll see something of themselves in you. Our Ideal Client would never consider using a large corporation. Because of their own entrepreneurial mindset, they naturally seem to resonate with our business model and want to champion and support us.

Recreation

What does your Ideal Client do for fun? Our clients are passionate about golf and, therefore, tend to have large homes within a short distance of a good club – it's no coincidence!

Dreams

This isn't the easiest topic to broach in an opening conversation, but if you learn to listen well, you'll be surprised at what people will tell you. You can start by asking a little bit about their long-term goals. Where do they see themselves in five years' time? On a beach in front of their holiday home or up a ladder refurbishing their Grade II listed mansion? How can you help them get there? Whatever your clients' dreams, putting them at the forefront of your marketing message will help you create a deeper connection and trust with them.

For a more in-depth version of this exercise and to download your free Ideal Client Avatar Worksheet, head to www.eliteagentcollective.com/resources or scan the QR code located on the back of this book.

Chapter 6
Your Lead Generation System

Building a System That Works,
Even When You Don't

Most agents only think about lead generation when their diary is empty, their inbox is quiet and their bank balance is looking nervously low.

But if you want to build a thriving, resilient, high-value estate agency, you can't afford to wait until things are quiet to start looking for your next client. Lead generation is not a panic button – it's a daily discipline.

The truth is this: You're not just in the business of selling homes. You're in the business of finding people who need to sell their homes, and convincing them that you're the one to do it brilliantly.

In this chapter, we'll walk you through the exact lead generation strategies we've used to build a £200m+ portfolio of listings, from letter-writing to door-knocking, social media to community building. We'll show you how to track the right numbers, avoid the ups and downs of feast and famine and create a steady, predictable pipeline of dream clients – without burning yourself out or becoming a content machine.

This is about doing less, *better*. Being smart, strategic and consistent. And, most of all, putting lead generation at the heart of your business, not at the bottom of your to-do list.

Let's get into it.

Which Lead Generation Method Should You Choose?

Different geographical areas and markets will respond differently to various marketing techniques, so in this chapter, we will focus on the lead generation methods that have proven effective for us in high-value homes.

The lead generation methods we are going to suggest to you are known to work particularly well with the top 25% of homes by value, which in our area of Oxfordshire tends to be homes valued over £1m. The types of people that own these homes don't tend to respond favourably to the sort of leaflets and flyers that you see from mid and low-end agents.

These homeowners are more discerning and therefore respond well to a marketing message that's more bespoke and offers something more than a "Free Valuation." (By the way, "Free Valuation" is just about the most outdated and over-used marketing message in our industry and it's about time we stopped relying on it as a sales tool. Of course, a valuation should be free! If anyone knows an agent that still charges we'd love to meet them!)

The strategies we are going to suggest to you form the basis of our own lead generation strategy which we have used to generate over £200m of listings over the last eight years. Importantly, they are all low-cost, high-impact strategies. Don't make the mistake of believing that you need to spend hundreds or thousands of pounds on the latest shiny piece of marketing software – just follow the simple strategies that we use daily in our business and work brilliantly, time and time again.

First Things First: Know Your Numbers

Before you embark on any lead generation activities, it's vitally important that you know your numbers! As recent converts to the joy of numbers and spreadsheets, we can categorically say that knowing the vital numbers and tracking the key metrics in your business will set you free, help you reach your goals, earn you more money, help you spot problems before they arise and thus help you sleep better at night.

The first key number you must decide upon is how much revenue you would like to make in the year. This is starting with the end in mind. After all, if you don't know where you're going how will you know when you've arrived? Once you know your target revenue number, you can work backwards from there to figure out how many sales you must complete on, how many homes you must get under offer, how many listings you must win, how many listing appointments you must go on and how many letters you must send out every month to ensure you generate enough listing appointments.

The equation looks like this:

Target Revenue = (Sales Completed) x (Homes Under Offer) x (Instructions Won) x (Listing Appointments Booked) x (Letters Sent per Month)

Let's say you'd like to earn £100,000 in 12 months in gross commission.

If your average fee per house sale is £5,000, you would need to complete on 20 home sales in 12 months to earn £100,000 in gross commission.

Then we need to factor in some other variables:

Currently, the fall-through rate of homes under offer in the UK is around 30%. To account for the number of homes that fall through, you would need to factor in some resilience and assume that some of your sales will fall through, thereby securing 26 homes under offer.

Now, this next number varies from region to region and at different price points, but last year, on average, only 54% of homes listed over £1m in Oxfordshire actually sold. So, in our business, we assume that only 1 out of every 2 homes we list will actually go on to complete a sale.

To reach 26 homes under offer, we would need to win 52 instructions and list 52 homes for sale on the market.

Now this is where you need to know your average conversion rate from listing appointment to instruction. Note: It is not "winning an instruction" when a prospect says to you, "We're not ready to sell yet, but we'll definitely use you when we are." Winning an instruction means actually getting a signed contract and putting a house on the market for sale.

It's no use applying vanity metrics here. Great-looking numbers might boost your ego, but they won't help you achieve your financial goals. On average, we are instructed on 50% of our listing appointments, but we think a good number to aim for is a conversion rate of anything over 30%. Whatever your number is, you must know it and track it so that you always know how many listing appointments you must book in your diary and complete.

So back to our numbers and our goal of reaching £100,000 in revenue. At a 50% valuation-to-instruction rate, to secure 52 instructions, we would need to attend 104 listing appointments over the year.

Before we break down that annual figure into a monthly goal, we need to factor in some holiday time (we're assuming you want to go on holiday and have some downtime throughout the year!), plus we need to take into account national bank holidays, Christmas and Easter. So, we divide the annual figure by 10 months rather than 12, giving you a monthly listing appointment target of just over 10 (10.4 to be exact!).

Now you know that to give you the best chance of hitting your £100,000 annual commission target you must book and complete at least 10 listing appointments *every single month*.

Your single most important job, before anything else, is to generate and carry out those listing appointments every month. Nothing else is a priority in your business until you have reached that number! Keep a weekly scorecard to ensure you're staying on track. You don't want to reach the last week of the month and realise you have only had two listing appointments.

Breaking down a seemingly daunting revenue and listing target into smaller, monthly amounts suddenly makes hitting your goals seem more achievable. And by learning to love the numbers in your business, and keeping track of them, you'll ensure you're consistently generating enough business to keep you off the scary Feast and Famine big dipper rollercoaster!

We work with all our franchisees on a one-to-one basis to map out their individual revenue goals for the year ahead and to plan their weekly, monthly and quarterly targets. If you'd like our help in creating a plan to achieve your dream revenue targets, we'd be delighted to offer you a complimentary 60-minute strategy and planning session. You can find our contact details in the "Reading and Resources List" section of this book.

Now that you know your numbers, let's take a look at the top lead generation strategies we use in our business to help us consistently reach the doors of £1m, £2m, £5m and even £10m+ homes. They are: direct mail, door knocking, social media and network and community building.

We'll explore all of these in detail in this chapter. But for now let's focus on our top-producing lead generation method: direct mail.

Lead Generation Strategy No. 1: Direct Mail

It would be no exaggeration to say that we have literally built our business on direct mail. On average, response rates to our direct mail campaigns are around 2% to 5%, a far better response rate than you'd expect from a leaflet campaign, which would be around 1 in 30,000. So, although our letter campaigns take quite a bit of effort and expense, the returns we receive are predictable and of exceptionally high quality.

At this point, we must credit two of our industry mentors: Sam Ashdown and Phil Jones, who run the incredible agency Ashdown Jones in the Lake District. Sam and Phil introduced us to the concept of direct mail for high-value homes. They helped us implement a high-value homes direct mail system, which has generated over £200m in listings for us.

We have now created our own direct mail system and write our own letters. Our franchisees utilise these as a key part of their lead generation, which has opened the doors to multi-million-pound homes for them in the first few months of their association with Stowhill Estates. For a detailed guide on direct mail, buy Sam Ashdown's excellent book *The Selective Estate Agent*.

To be absolutely clear: Direct mail is *not* sending out tens of thousands of leaflets that land on the doormat next to the Dominoes discount flyer. Nor is it about hiring companies to send generic, one-page automated letters to homes already on the market at pre-set trigger points in their selling journey.

Our very special (and highly effective) version of direct mail involves targeting a very select group of homeowners, both on and off the market, and sending them a long-form, carefully curated and professionally copywritten letter. This letter either offers specific advice for selling their home on the market or a regular market update about how the high-value homes market is performing in their area.

Why Does Direct Mail Work?

In this digital age, we are bombarded daily with emails, texts and WhatsApp messages. Just take a moment to think about how many emails you receive on an average day. And of those how many are junk?

We receive around 100 per day of which at least 50% are from some sort of mailing list that we may or may not have signed up to. With so many emails landing in our inbox on a daily basis, it's easy just to ignore them and send them to the bin without ever opening them.

But now think about the last time you received an actual letter through your door, with a handwritten address and stamp, presented in a high-quality envelope? Maybe it was on your birthday? Or maybe, if you're lucky, it was Valentine's Day?

The point is this: Letters that aren't bills are becoming so rare these days that when one drops through your letterbox, it immediately gets your attention.

A premium-looking piece of mail that drops through the door, with the address hand-written in ink, will be more likely to be opened. It creates a sense of quality and intrigue. When the content inside is carefully written, tailored specifically to the homeowner and offering useful, relevant information, it is far more likely to elicit a favourable response. This moves a prospect closer to working with you.

What Should My Letters Say?

If you've ever had your home on the market or worked for a corporate estate agency, you'll already know that the vast majority of estate agents touting letters and leaflets all contain messaging which is a variation on the same theme:

"We have sold more homes in your area than any other agent."

"We have buyers waiting for homes like yours."

"We can give you a free, no-obligation valuation."

"We are No.1 on Rightmove."

"We have won 20 industry awards."

Etc. etc.

It still amazes us that these lazy, generic marketing messages still work. Did you notice that none of the messages above are about the seller? They're all about the agent: how great they are or how many homes they've sold. This is what most agents do with their marketing (and on valuations, for that matter!). They talk only about themselves, never listen properly or tailor their service to what the seller might want or need.

There have been hundreds of books written on the art of persuasive sales letter writing. For a simple, no-nonsense and brilliant book, we'd recommend anything by Dan Kennedy, but particularly a simple, easy-to-read book called *The Ultimate Sales Letter*.

If you've never written sales copy before, the prospect of sitting down and writing an interesting, persuasive and informative letter might seem a bit daunting. But we want to reassure you that there are just a few key steps to writing persuasive and compelling copy.

The key to a great sales letter is keeping the focus on the reader, not the writer. It's about making the reader feel understood rather than bombarding them with facts and figures and boasts about how great you and your agency are. People won't necessarily remember exactly what you said, but they will remember how you made them feel. Helping them feel understood is a crucial first step in creating a persuasive sales letter.

Whilst we're on this subject, can we just turn to industry awards? At the risk of upsetting you, we want to share a harsh truth, and we're going to be direct because we care. *No one cares about your industry awards except you.* There, we said it! Winning an industry award might be a great confidence boost for you and your team, and possibly a great night out too, but using them as a sales tactic is completely pointless. It's likely that your prospective seller won't understand what the award is about and even more likely that they won't actually care.

So, now we've got that out of the way, let's look at the framework for a great sales letter.

Make It Long

This might seem counterintuitive, as you might think that people receiving correspondence from you want you to get straight to the point. However, research has shown that the longer someone engages with your content, the more likely they are to take an action. In this case, the action you want them to take is to reach out to you to book a home consultation. Sure, there will be people who just skim through or put your letter straight into the bin, but for those who do read it, the message will likely resonate more deeply. Our letters are typically 4 to 6 pages long and contain various font types, sizes, pictures, case studies and testimonials, designed to keep the reader engaged for as long as possible.

Keep It Personal

Although you want your letter to be well structured with correct spelling and grammar, you also want to include some of your personality, so use conversational language rather than overly formal words and phrases and include a picture of yourself so people can see who is writing to them and get to know you early on (Pro tip: Ditch the corporate headshot and include a picture of you outside of work on holiday or with your family). Tailor your language to resonate with their situation. You might want to mention specifics about their property or about current market challenges to help build trust and rapport.

Follow a Structure

It's useful to follow a specific letter structure every time and then allow your authentic personality to shine through over the top of the structure. A time honoured letter format is:

1. Tell them what you're going to tell them in the letter.
2. Tell them.
3. Tell them what you've told them.

Start With a Headline

Unlike a formal "Dear sir or madam,"-type letter, we always start all our letters with a bold headline designed to capture the reader's attention. This is your chance to craft a punchy and powerful message that will stop the reader in their tracks and spark enough interest and intrigue for them to continue reading the letter. The headline sets the tone for the rest of your letter so it's worth investing some time to make it compelling. Our opening headlines often take the form of a question, such as:

"Why do some homes take so long to sell?"

"Why is my home not selling?"

"What do I need to do to ensure I sell my home before Christmas?"

Or you could try using a powerful, benefit-driven statement that uses strong, active language and promises a proven result. Dan Kennedy refers to the headline as the "doorway" to the rest of the message. Some examples we've used in the past:

"Discover the secret to selling your home on your terms."

"Unlock the power of bespoke marketing to sell your home faster, and for more."

"Revealing the top ten secrets to a fast home sale."

Paragraph 1: Acknowledge Their Situation

Showing empathy early on in the letter and demonstrating that you understand what they're going through will put you on a good footing to encourage them to read on. You might open your letter with something like this:

"If your house is currently sitting on the market with no viewings, or you've had viewings but no offers, you're probably feeling frustrated and wondering what else you can do to encourage more buyer interest."

Paragraph 2: Reassurance

So, you've acknowledged the reader's situation and demonstrated that you understand what they're going through. The next step is to reassure them that they are not alone, it's not their fault, that many other people have found themselves in similar situations and that help is at hand. You can then advise them to continue reading to discover the solution to their problem.

"If you're feeling disappointed, frustrated or even misled by your current agent's promises, you're not alone. Many sellers in Oxfordshire find themselves stuck with a home that isn't selling, wondering what went wrong.

The truth? Selling a high-value home takes more than just listing it online and waiting. It requires a strategic, results-driven approach to attract the right buyers and close the deal efficiently."

Paragraph 3: Identify Their Problem and Amplify Their Pain

At this point in your letter, you're going to gently, but firmly, shine a spotlight on what the consequences might be if the reader doesn't sell their home. What will their pain points be? They'll lose time, they might miss out on the home they want to buy, they'll feel stressed and they'll lose money if they do nothing now and need to drop the price later.

We know you don't want to come across as the sleazy estate agent, and you don't want to manipulate them or play on their worst fears, but you do want to subtly reiterate what might happen if they don't take action now to solve their problem.

"Many sellers are stuck waiting for the 'right buyer' while precious months slip by. The truth is that the longer a home sits on the market, the lower your chance of achieving your desired asking price. Selling a high-value home requires a strategic approach which involves much more than just listing it online and waiting."

Paragraph 4: Be the Hero!

Now you've identified your prospect's biggest pain point and empathised with their situation, it's time to introduce your unique solution. This is your cue to step up and become the hero! You've successfully identified the gap between the reader's current reality and where they want to be. Your solution is now the bridge between these two islands.

This is your chance to really highlight why your solution is unique and completely different to the competition. At this point, we sometimes include a sentence that acknowledges that the reader might feel they've heard it all before, offering further reassurance that our solution really is different.

We might say something like, "I know what you're thinking: all estate agents are the same! But please allow me to demonstrate how we do things differently and why I think our unique selling process could be the key to finally unlocking your successful home sale."

Be very specific in this paragraph about the things that set you apart. This is the time to present your unique selling process and the things you do that other agents can't and won't.

"At Stowhill Estates, we specialise in helping homeowners just like you get unstuck, take back control of their property sale and sell for the price they want, in the timescale they need, using our "7 Steps to Sold" system.

This takes a proactive and tailored approach to unique home sales and includes:

Bespoke lifestyle marketing. Video tours, lifestyle photography and professionally written descriptions, proven to generate more buyer interest and elicit higher offers.

Marketing beyond Rightmove. We actively target 'passive buyers' and those not actively searching on property portals through off-market marketing campaigns, liaison with national and international buying agents, and through our VIP Buyers' Club.

Expert negotiation. Our negotiation results in our clients achieving an average of 104% of their original asking price."

Paragraph 5: Prove it!

This is a great point in your letter to introduce a case study or testimonial to back up your claims. A great case study takes the form of a story. Think of someone who has been in a similar situation before, then met you and was introduced to your solution. Initially, they weren't sure it would work, but after taking a leap of faith, finally achieved a great result through working with you.

Use facts and data here to endorse your claims. (This should go without saying but never, ever make it up! You don't want to destroy all your hard-earned credibility in one sentence.) This is the place to shout about your achievements, whether it's selling homes faster than other agents, achieving a higher sale price or fewer sales falling through.

A great case study might read something like this:

> "John and Sarah's beautiful home had been sat on the market for 18 long months with their previous estate agent, and when they finally reached out to us, having missed out on the chance to offer on three homes they wanted to buy, they were feeling frustrated, confused and thoroughly demoralised by the whole home-selling process.
>
> When we visited them at their beautiful home, it was clear that the problem lay not with their property, but with the marketing. Their original photos were taken by the agent on their phone, were not professionally lit or edited and did not fully showcase the lifestyle of this wonderful house.

There was no video tour to offer potential buyers enticing glimpses of the key rooms and grounds, and the description was bland and unengaging, merely listing the rooms and their square footage.

John and Sarah were on the verge of giving up on the whole thing and staying put for another year. However, after calling us in for a personalised marketing audit and home consultation, we managed to convince them that our unique strategies could help them relaunch their home to a new audience, stimulate refreshed buyer interest, and sell their home within their desired timeframe. Somewhat reluctantly, they agreed to give it one last go.

Just six weeks later, we're delighted to say that John and Sarah were Under Offer to a cash buyer who was relocating from London to their dream family home in the Oxfordshire countryside, and who paid over the asking price to secure the property. The sale was completed in another six weeks, and John and Sarah were able to finally move to the south coast to be closer to their grandchildren."

Paragraph 6: Sell the Sizzle, Not the Sausage

Or to put it another way: Emphasise the benefits of working with you over the features. What will the reader gain by working with you and engaging all the features you offer? When you're writing this paragraph, you might want to keep in mind, "What's in it for the client?" For example, you might offer video tours as part of your marketing package. Instead of just saying, "We offer professionally filmed video tours," tell the reader why you do it and how it benefits them. For example:

"We offer professionally filmed and produced 4K video tours as standard because we know that homes with a video receive 400% more buyer enquiries than those without, and sell 50% faster on average."

Make sure you translate every feature into a tangible benefit for the client, so that features go from "nice to have" to "absolutely essential."

Paragraph 7: Present Your Irresistible Offer

Dan Kennedy advises that every great sales letter must include a low-risk, high-reward offer that makes it easy for a prospect to say yes:

"I'd love to offer you a complimentary personalised Home Marketing Audit where we can review the reasons why your home hasn't sold and provide customised strategies to help you take back control of your home sale. There's absolutely no cost or commitment from your side (other than about an hour of your time and a cuppa!). At the end of our meeting, you'll have some actionable insights from a proven expert on how to get your home sold quickly and for the best price."

Paragraph 8: Create a Compelling Call to Action

You'd be surprised how many people write a brilliant sales letter and then completely forget the most important part:

Telling the reader what you'd like them to do next! Make sure you include a clear, simple call to action and make it easy for them to get in touch with you with minimal obligation or risk.

It's also a good idea to create some urgency in your call to action. You don't want the reader to put your letter away in a drawer and then forget about it. So, make your offer time-bound and with limited availability to encourage them to take action immediately.

You might say something like:

"To ensure the best results, we only work with a limited number of clients at any one time and our home consultation slots fill up very quickly. If you'd like to take advantage of one of the remaining slots for April, you can call or WhatsApp me directly at (Number)."

Paragraph 9: Don't Forget the PS!

You might be surprised to hear that many readers skip straight to the P.S., or just skim-read through the main content. Including a P.S. at the end of the letter will ensure you capture the attention of these skimmers! The P.S. is your opportunity to summarise your letter in a nutshell and reiterate the call to action.

"P.S. Homes in Oxfordshire that aren't marketed strategically often sit on the market far too long, leading to price reductions and lost profits. Don't let that happen to yours. Call me today at [phone number] to see how we can turn things around quickly!"

You could also consider including a special offer or bonus in the P.S. that sweetens the deal. A free twilight or drone photograph, for example, or a bonus video or reel for social media.

This sales letter framework has helped us create hundreds of compelling and high-performing sales letters over the past eight years, resulting in the sale of hundreds of high-value homes. We hope this step-by-step guide helps you to create your own. Don't forget to add your own personality so that the readers get to know the authentic you!

Writing compelling copy is one of our greatest loves, and we are delighted to write a fantastic market sales letter for our Stowhill Estates franchisees and Elite Agent Mastermind members every month. Please feel free to reach out to us if you'd like us to review your sales letters and offer tips and advice. Lucy in particular loves a good sales letter, so feel free to email her at lucy@stowhillestates.com.

Lead Generation Strategy No. 2: Door Knocking

Love it or hate it, door-knocking is undoubtedly the most effective way to get results *quickly*. Some agents swear by it and use it as their key lead-generation strategy. For others, the mere thought of knocking on a stranger's door and asking for their business leaves them with a feeling of sheer terror!

You might be one of these second group of people who would rather stick pins in their eyes than door knock. But before you dismiss it altogether, consider this: Our partner agents have all secured their first-ever multi-million pound listings from door knocking, and their average success rate for converting a door knock into an instruction is around 4 out of 10. It takes them around 2 hours to knock on 10 doors. With an average house price of £1.5m and an average fee of £22,000, that's a pretty good hourly rate!

Many agents tell us they don't want to door-knock because they don't know what to say and are worried they'll get tongue-tied and look stupid. As with all lead generation tools, it really helps to have a process. So for those of you who quite fancy the idea of ringing the doorbells of high-value homes, here are our top tips on how to do it, when to do it and what to say.

What Is Door Knocking?

Door knocking is when you show up on the doorstep of a select few homes you have earmarked as being on the market and unsold, where you would like to encourage them to change agents and take on their instruction. Don't overthink it – all you're doing is introducing yourself and asking if and how you can help the homeowner.

The purpose of the door knock is not to be invited in and conduct the home consultation immediately. In fact, we would strongly advise against doing this, even if the homeowner is insistent that you come in and take a look around. However, this approach often catches people off guard and does not put you or the seller in the best frame of mind for a productive conversation. The purpose of the door knock is to arrange a time for you to return for a home consultation, where you can guide and advise them on strategies to sell their home.

Write to Them First

Only consider a door knock on a home if you have already sent them at least three letters without getting a response. The element of surprise won't work in your favour here! Instead, you want to increase the chance that they've seen and read your letters, and recognise you from your photos. We've found in our experience that the conversion rate from door-knocking increases dramatically when they have already received some content from you and engaged with your brand in some way.

It's important to keep in mind that just because they haven't responded to your letter so far doesn't mean that they're not interested in working with you. There may be a hundred different reasons why they haven't picked up the phone yet, the simplest being that maybe they're just not ready. Believe it or not, inertia is a strategy for many homeowners whose homes aren't selling.

Sometimes people would rather just sit and do nothing and hope that a buyer comes along, than admit they need to take action and change strategy. The purpose of your visit at this stage is therefore just to gently nudge and guide them towards considering changing agents. You may find (as we often do) that they have kept all your letters and that they are safely filed away for future reference. (Our record is 9 letters sent before a homeowner called us!)

Door Knocking Strategies

Weekdays and early evenings are generally the best time to catch people at home. Between 4 pm and 6 pm is a good time. Don't leave it too late, as people will be having dinner. It should go without saying that you shouldn't door-knock too early, especially on the weekend.

When introducing yourself, don't worry about memorising a clever script or hundreds of facts and figures. You're simply there to introduce yourself:

"Hello, my name is Lucy from Stowhill Estates Unique Homes. You might have noticed that I've sent you a few letters over the past few weeks. I was in the area, so I wanted to come and introduce myself and see if and how I can help you."

It's really as simple as that. Many people (particularly high-value homeowners) will spot the entrepreneurial spirit in you and might praise your persistence and tenacity. Don't assume that every door will be slammed in your face – you might be pleasantly surprised how many positive responses you get!

Many of our partner agents have had great success with delivering a gift of some sort to the homeowner. This could be a box of brownies, some chocolates, a potted plant, Easter eggs or even Christmas puddings. These can be hand-delivered alongside an unapologetic note saying something like:

"Hi! We've sent you four letters and still haven't received a reply, so we're unashamedly trying to bribe you to pick up the phone with these cakes. If it's not obvious already, we'd absolutely love to help you sell your home! While you're enjoying these cakes/brownies, please dial my number into your phone (it's 01234-5678-7891). I'll be waiting for your call. Best wishes, Lucy Joerin."

Keep it fun and light-hearted, as the aim is to be memorable and interesting. Don't forget that this is something that your competitors can't and likely won't do, so if you're willing to get out of your comfort zone a little bit and go after the market, the rewards can be incredible. If you do decide to take the plunge into door-knocking, we'd love to know how you get on! Go get 'em!

Lead Generation Strategy No. 3: Social Media and Content

One of the great things about the rise of social media is that it serves as a great leveller. In the 21st century, we all have the same access to an audience of potential sellers and buyers as the big corporate agencies do, without the need to spend thousands of pounds on advertising. What's more, as independent agents we can be agile and dynamic, adopting new strategies and tactics quickly without having to wait for the approval of endless levels of corporate bureaucracy.

Social media and the internet have also negated the need for agents to have a physical office. We no longer need the hassle and expense of a high-street shop window to gain visibility. We can reach thousands of potential clients through the click of a button, which is a tremendously exciting opportunity for independent agents!

There's never been a more exciting time to generate brand awareness, get your message across to your target audience effectively and build raving fans of you and your business through content creation. High-quality and engaging content has the added bonus of enabling you to build rapport and trust with your prospective customers. It's a beautiful way to show your authenticity and demonstrate your knowledge and expertise to the exact audience who needs you.

You can also use content to effectively reach homeowners who are just beginning to consider selling their homes. On average, sellers begin their thought process about moving around 18 months before they actually pick up the phone to appoint an agent. Ensuring you are "top of mind" during that 18-month "consideration" period will put you in the prime position to be invited in for a home consultation when they're ready to move.

There are a number of ways that you can create content, and several different platforms that you can use to reach your desired audience – anything from TikTok to LinkedIn and everything in between. You might decide to create detailed video guides, 30-second market updates, quick "home sellers tricks and tips" reels, written guidebooks, checklists, podcasts or infographics. The options and opportunities are endless.

Be warned, however, that it's precisely because we have all of these options that often we don't post consistently enough and in the right way, or don't post or create content at all because it's all too overwhelming. Here we come back to the strategy: Consistency is key when creating content and posting on social media, so it's important for you to develop a content and social media strategy that ensures you are regularly posting the right content on the right platforms to reach your desired outcomes.

You don't have to post on every platform, but choose the ones where your audience is most active. If you haven't yet completed your Ideal Client Persona template (which you can download by scanning the QR code located on the back of this book), we encourage you to revisit it and create a profile of your perfect client, allowing you to understand which online and social media platforms they're most likely to use.

Through developing our ideal client persona, we discovered that our client base is most likely to be on LinkedIn, as they tend to be senior-level management or entrepreneurs. They're a slightly older demographic, so they prefer Facebook and occasionally use Instagram as well. We prioritise posting on these platforms over others, such as TikTok, which tend to attract a younger demographic.

Of course, in an ideal world, you'd be posting everywhere all the time, but for most people this is unrealistic. We're going to guess that you don't have a full-time social media team at your disposal, so focus your efforts on creating content tailored to your ideal client persona and posting regularly across the platforms where they're most likely to be.

Your website should also form a cornerstone of your content strategy. If you own and manage your own website (and are not part of a larger self-employed group, such as Exp or Keller Williams), then you should regularly post high-quality and engaging long-form content in the form of a blog post on your website, at least once a month. This will significantly boost your SEO and provide a basis for creating shorter pieces of content from the original blog, which you can use across your chosen social media platforms.

It's estimated that it can take anywhere from 7 to 12 "touch points" whereby a prospect engages with your brand in several different ways before making a decision to work with you. So ensuring you maximise your visibility online is critical in generating awareness and trust for you and your brand. By the way, you'll know you've got this right when a prospect says to you, "I keep seeing you everywhere!" The reality is they may have seen one of your For Sale boards, read a Facebook post, watched one of your property videos or engaged with some advice content on your website, but their perception is that you are omnipresent – which puts you in prime position to be their agent of choice!

Lead Generation Strategy No. 4: Networking and Community Building

Some of our partner agents' biggest listings have come from networking, with £5m, £7m and even £10m instructions won by our agents as a result of both networking and getting out and about in the local community. In fact, in terms of a strategy to win super-prime instructions, it's hard to beat networking.

In the prime property space, it's as much about who you know as what you know, so spending time building connections with high-net-worth individuals and the service providers they use is worth spending some time on. As one of our mentors, Matt Elwell, is fond of saying: "The more you connect, the more you collect."

Many people dread the idea of networking, and I'm sure we've all been to one of those networking meetings where you have to show up at 6 am every week and take turns standing up to deliver a 30-second pitch to the group. It makes us shudder too! But the good news is that networking doesn't have to be boring or pressurised. In fact, it is really possible to have fun and make new friends whilst building business connections at the same time.

It's all about how you network. Just like going to the gym, it's a good habit that you'll only continue if you enjoy it. So, make it a priority to find a networking or community-building strategy that you actually enjoy – there are loads around! Believe it or not, you can network whilst playing sports like golf or netball, or attending supper clubs and wine tastings or joining walking groups. You definitely don't have to sit in a cold village hall on a Monday morning!

Traditional networking and community building are two distinct tactics aimed at achieving the same end goal: connecting with as many people and complementary businesses as possible. Both work exceptionally well when done correctly, but you may find that you prefer one strategy over the other. Let's explore the difference between the two:

Networking

Networking, essentially, is about regularly getting out into the community you serve to share training and best practices, pass and refer business, and make mutually beneficial connections with individuals and local businesses.

As well as generating potential seller leads for you, networking can also be a fantastic source of supplier contacts for your business. We have found our accountant, printer, social media consultant, website developer and car finance broker all through networking. It's a great feeling when you can pass business and referrals to one another, utilise services within the group, and support each other's small businesses.

A networking event usually takes the format of time at the start to informally chat and meet each other, followed by a 30- or 60-second pitch to the group where you have a chance to introduce yourself and your business formally and ask for referrals. Sometimes, a networking group will have a guest speaker, a training or business workshop session and occasionally, a member of the group will have a longer speaking opportunity to present their business.

A quick Google search will bring up hundreds of different networking groups to try in your local area. As with dating, if you're new to networking, you may need to try out a few before you decide on "the one." Our favourites are the nationwide "Fore" Business groups which combine networking with a round of golf, and a local Oxfordshire supper club that gives you the chance to meet and connect with other entrepreneurs and businesses whilst trying out a different local restaurant every month.

Community Building

Essentially, community building is a form of networking where you're in control. You run the business group or the event, invite the members and set the agenda. For control freaks like us, it's a great way to get out and be visible in our local business community without having to join someone else's group. It's also a great way to showcase your particular skill set.

Create Your Own Club

A great way to gain visibility in your community is by establishing your own community club. This could be a business club or a hobby-based group, such as a running club, book club or supper club. We set up our own Marketing Club, which provided a regular monthly workshop for local small businesses and entrepreneurs. Lucy's background in PR and Marketing gave her a fantastic opportunity to showcase her expertise in this area and position herself as a property marketing expert.

Although you can set up any type of community club, a business-based group is an ideal way to connect with your target audience as well as the types of people that will refer you to your target clients.

It's a great way to position yourself as a community business leader and to become a trusted and valued member of your local business community. As you are front and centre it's a far more powerful way to gain visibility and influence than networking at someone else's event. Plus it can be really fun!

Keep it small and simple to start with. Find a suitable venue (such as a village hall, meeting room at a local business centre or your local golf club) and pick a day to host your event. We find that mid-week mornings are best. You want to aim for a 2-3 hour workshop with time for coffee and tea in the middle and perhaps informal networking afterwards. It's a good idea to charge a small amount for the event, to cover your costs and to gain a level of commitment from the attendees. Anything between £5 and £10 is a good amount. We recommend selling tickets to the event in advance on a platform like Eventbrite, so you can get a good idea of the numbers.

Then, post on your personal Facebook, LinkedIn or Instagram page to announce that you are running a monthly club. Set up a member's Facebook page where you can post all the event details, as well as any other announcements for the group, between your monthly meetings. This is another fantastic way to build a powerful Facebook following that you can communicate with regularly and position yourself as a key person of influence in your community.

Local Business Spotlight

Get noticed within your local community by becoming a local business champion and supporter. Industry guru Christopher Watkin calls this tactic becoming a "Digital Mayor," where "digital" refers to online and "mayor" refers to someone who is important within the local community.

This is another low-cost, high-impact strategy that will rapidly build "know, like and trust" collateral in your business. Our partner agents in Marlow, David and Sara, used this tactic with enormous success when they first launched their business. They selected twelve local, independent businesses and filmed short interviews with each of the founders, highlighting the businesses and giving them a festive visibility boost. Alongside this, they ran a local daily giveaway with each business in the run-up to Christmas. A new interview and giveaway was hosted on their business Facebook page every day, gaining them a huge instant Facebook following from a standing start and bagging them a £4m instruction to boot.

Despite the fact that neither David nor Sara actually live in Marlow, the impact of this campaign was so great that they regularly get recognised walking down Marlow High Street and have built up a large following and an even larger bucket of goodwill in the local community.

The cost to them? No more than a few hours of their time and a few pounds spent on Facebook to "boost" the first few posts. Minimal investment and maximum return! It's something that any of the local Marlow estate agents could have done at some point over the past twenty or so years they've been on the high street, but the fact that very few agents will actually invest the time or effort to do this gives you an enormous advantage over the competition.

Why not run your own local regular local business spotlight on Facebook? It's free and gives you the chance to regularly get out and about within your local community, meet local business owners who will recommend and refer you and support their businesses at the same time. It's a win-win for everyone.

Alternatively, you could look for a community project to get involved with. Whether it's a local litter pick, fundraising for a new playground or supporting local charities, it's an opportunity to raise awareness of you and your brand as a key figure within your local area.

If you love eating and drinking, consider reviewing local coffee shops, pubs or restaurants to visit and recommend. As a family, we love going out for Sunday lunch and regularly post pictures of our Sunday roasts on our social media! You could act like a local news reporter and share details of local events, such as country fairs, festivals, fireworks events, school or village fetes, etc.

It's about thinking outside the box of estate agency and property and raising your profile within the local community so that you are top of mind when they come to choose an agent or when someone asks for a referral.

Consistency is key, so however you choose to raise your profile within your local community, make sure it's something you genuinely enjoy doing so that there's a good chance you'll keep it going! And don't forget to be your authentic self. Don't overthink it or try and be too polished or scripted – this is your chance for people to get to know the real you!

Finally, don't forget to regularly review and measure your lead generation activities to ensure they're working consistently for you.

Let the System Do the Heavy Lifting for You

The golden rule of lead generation is that it only works if you do it consistently.

You now have a blueprint for building a reliable, scalable system to fill your diary with high-value listing appointments, all without begging, cold-calling or burning out. Whether you lean into direct mail, door-knocking, social media, community networking or all of the above, the secret lies not in the tactic itself, but in your ability to stick with it.

Track your numbers. Know your targets. Celebrate your wins. Refine what's not working. Above all: Make lead generation the non-negotiable heartbeat of your business.

Because when you build a lead generation machine that works even when you're on holiday, at a photo shoot or celebrating another successful exchange, you create freedom. Freedom to choose your clients. Freedom to grow at your pace. Freedom to build a business that supports your life and not the other way around.

Lead generation isn't just a task. It's your ticket to a bigger, better and more joyful business.

So go get started. Your future clients are out there waiting for you to show up.

Chapter 7
The Art of the "Yes"

Winning Instructions With Ease and Elegance

Most agents treat the listing appointment like a performance. The slick suit, the flashy brochure, the well-rehearsed pitch. But the more you try to convince, the less trust you build. And in the high-value homes market, trust isn't a bonus; it's the whole game.

In this chapter, we will help you stop pitching and start partnering. You'll learn how to flip the script and turn what most agents see as a sales presentation into a meaningful strategy conversation. One that's rooted in connection, trust, and clarity, rather than desperate persuasion.

We'll show you how to win the listing even when you're not the cheapest, not the biggest and not the highest valuation. Why? Because when you approach the listing appointment with purpose, process and presence, your ideal clients will feel it. They'll choose you because of who you *are*, not just what you *say*.

What follows is the exact mindset, method and messaging we've used to win high-value instructions time and time again, not by being sales-y, but by being genuine. This is the art of winning the listing, the Elite Agent way.

As an agent, your business lives or dies by your ability to create leads (people with homes to sell) and then convert those leads into instructions that you can sell and make money, thereby reaching your financial goals.

You have to develop your superpower to win people's trust so that they believe that you are the only person who can get them from where they are now to where they want to go.

Most estate agents we've met believe that the estate agent who gives the highest valuation and the lowest fee is the most likely to win the listing.

We're going to ask you to suspend your disbelief for just one moment and suggest to you that it is absolutely possible to win the listing 9 times out of 10 even if you are the most expensive agent, even if you are the lowest valuation and even if you are the only one charging an up-front marketing fee.

How do we know? Well, because we do it ourselves. And our partner agents do it, too (some of them admittedly didn't come from an agency background, so they didn't have any bad habits to unlearn!) We practice what we preach, and we would never, ever suggest that you do something that we are not 100% confident works.

In this chapter, we'll share with you our secrets to winning the trust and belief of your ideal client. We'll show you how to turn valuations into home consultations, where, instead of pitching for the business, you have an elegant and effortless strategy conversation with your clients.

You're Not Meant to Win Every Instruction

The whole process of winning the listing starts with you going to home consultations with the people whom you have already identified as your ideal clients *only*. If you have been through the Ideal Client exercise and know exactly what type of client you want to work with (and who you don't), then at your listing appointment, you'll likely be sitting with the perfect prospect in their sitting room.

If you haven't completed your Ideal Client exercise, we urge you to go back and do so. This process works so much better when you know you are only talking to people who are already more than 90% sure they are going to work with you because they have "opted in." And those prospects that don't "get" what you do have already self-selected themselves out, so you don't need to waste your time trying to persuade people who are never going to buy from you.

Here's a key mindset shift you'll need:

You are not meant to win every instruction.

In case you didn't take that last sentence in, we'll repeat it for you here:

You are not meant to win every instruction.

That's right. You are not supposed to win every time. This was hard for both of us to hear and really understand at first, and it may be hard for you, too, if you're a naturally competitive person. (If we ever meet in person, dear reader, ask Michael about the first time we went on holiday with Lucy's family, and a huge row erupted over a game of Trivial Pursuit!)

But once you let go of the need to "win" every time and at any cost, it opens up a beautiful pathway to exploring whether you can really help this client, with no pressure and no hard sell needed. You'll shift your mindset from "I'd better win this instruction, or else I won't do my number this month and I won't make any money and the kids will starve" to "Let me go and meet this person and spend an hour or two with them asking about their life and their plans and discovering if and how I can help them." Sounds great, doesn't it? Pressure off. Stress levels lowered. Mind open to discovery. And breathe...

With this mindset, *you* are in control. You're not doing an X-Factor audition! You are choosing whether the client is a good fit for you at the same time as they are choosing whether you are a good fit for them.

If it's a win-win for both of you, then the next steps to working together will feel natural and easy. If not, that's fine, too. You can lovingly release them to find an agent that will better suit their needs. And this requires a second mindset shift:

There is enough business available for everyone, and there are *always* opportunities to be found.

It's not a zero-sum game.

Estate agents are natural people pleasers. We can't help it, it's just in our nature. We want everyone to like us, and we want to be a superhero for everyone.

It's why when we lose an instruction, it feels really personal. You wonder what you did or said wrong, and then you put it down to the fact that the other agent must have given them a higher valuation and a lower fee.

But taking every lost instruction personally can really hinder your progress and knock your confidence. I'll never forget the time we were called in to value a fantastic home back in 2019 in the early days of our business. We had sold a similar home down the road, and the seller had spotted our board.

We visited this amazing property just before Christmas. We tried very hard to keep our cool as we walked around this 5,000 sq ft mansion with two acres that had just been renovated from top to bottom, including a £100,000 kitchen. The owners were full of praise for the great job we had done selling the house down the road and loved the way we marketed and presented homes.

They were enthusiastic and keen for us to sell their home too, and as soon as possible. They just needed to get a few odd jobs completed before Christmas, and then they'd be ready to go in the new year. We left on a handshake (our favourite "old-school" way of doing business) and drove home buzzing with excitement and looking forward to the new year when we could get the photos and video taken.

Imagine our shock and surprise, waking up on New Year's Day and opening Facebook to find the same house, in all its glory, on a super-sexy video...*for sale with another agent.*

We literally couldn't believe it. So much for "my word is my bond"! We won't go into the whys and wherefores here, or what we could and should have done to secure the instruction before Christmas (suffice it to say that there were some big lessons for us here).

The real challenge was that it emotionally knocked us for six. It would not be an exaggeration to say that Lucy spent three full days in bed crying. Not only had we taken the loss of the instruction personally, but it was also the only opportunity we had secured in December, leaving us financially exposed as well.

But as with every seemingly shitty situation that happens (they always feel super-shitty at the time don't they?), there was a lesson contained within the experience that was essential for our business and personal growth. So, in hindsight, we can say we're grateful for this gift (amongst many others that we'd rather not have experienced at the time!).

And the lesson is: Winning or losing the instruction is never personal. If you continue to think that way, it will hold you back. Estate agency is a numbers game; if you're playing the numbers right, you are going to hear the word "no" an awful lot. Get used to losing, get used to hearing "no," even expect it. Heck, why not celebrate it? "I had ten listing appointments this month, and five said no!" Great! Guess what that means? Five said, "Yes!"

One of our good friends and fellow agents, Benjamin Scrace, compares this mindset to holding a pack of cards in which you're trying to find the two Jokers. There are 52 cards in the deck. Every card you turn over that's not the Joker brings you closer to finding it. Every time you hear "no" in a home consultation, you're one step closer to hearing a "yes."

Forecasting how many no's you're likely to get takes away the elements of surprise and disappointment. Although our conversion rate is currently closer to 70%, we still forecast winning only 50% of instructions.

Remember that is just a number, and there's safety in numbers.

What a Shift in Mindset Can Do

We had a coaching client who hated doing valuations and home consultations. She used to say to us, "I don't know what to say; I can't memorise it all." She ran the business with her partner, who was an absolute genius at presenting as well as memorising facts and figures.

Because this agent was in the mindset that she had to "sell," she felt like a spare part in the valuation. She lost her confidence because she didn't know what to say, and as a result, stopped going out to valuations completely. This was really a tragedy because what she didn't realise (although we're happy to say she realises it now) was that she actually had superpowers of listening, empathising and a unique and incredible ability to make her prospects feel understood. And guess what people do when they feel truly understood? That's right: They buy!

By not going out to the valuation appointment, this amazing agent was unwittingly depriving her potential clients of the opportunity to be listened to, heard and understood.

Our Framework to Help You Land the Listing Every Time

Have you ever noticed how some people seem to effortlessly make sales, win instructions, and make it all look easy? Whilst others struggle, fumble, stumble and occasionally screw it up royally?

The most successful agents (and salespeople) we know all follow a process. Your sales process begins the moment you or your team picks up the phone to call a prospect or answers an email or text. Whilst it may take some time to create and refine, once you've nailed this process, we know you'll find the sales part easier and even enjoyable, because it will feel less like an audition and more like a conversation.

Plus, at some point in your business, you may want to grow your team. Creating a sales process will allow you the freedom to build your business by having your team go out and smash those listing appointments for you.

Creating your unique sales process will give you an effortless and elegant sales system that is repeatable, teachable and authentic to you. It creates confidence in you when you enter the valuation, and certainty in your prospect that working with you is the right decision.

We're going to teach you a simple framework that we use ourselves in every home consultation. By using this framework as your anchor, you can make sure that speaking to prospects in their own home feels natural and effortless, and helps you win the listing.

The formula we use is called L.A.N.D.S, and it's been created to give you the very best chance that every instruction LANDS in your lap. (See what we did there?)

It stands for Listen, Ask, Needs, Demonstration and Steps.

Did you know that people make buying decisions using two parts of their brain: the logical side and the emotional side? Most agents think that appealing to the logical side is the way to make a sale. And so their listing presentations contain a long list of facts and figures, including data on the number of houses they've sold and the amount of commission they've earned. Agents falsely believe that this is what their prospect wants to hear. But they couldn't be more wrong.

Many agents do this in their sales pitches, on their websites and on their social media. Here are a few random sentences we picked out after a couple of Google searches of top agents in the country:

"We have years of experience in selling homes."

"We are senior property professionals."

"I am the leading luxury estate agent in the UK."

"We are highly skilled experts."

"I am a leading authority in high-end real estate."

"We have won an industry Gold award for the most sales."

Sorry to be harsh, but so what? We hate to tell you, but when a prospect is looking for someone to help them sell their home, the only question they have in their mind is, "What's in it for me?" So, don't be like most agents who make it all about themselves. Flip the switch and tailor the home consultation process to make it all about them. It's easy if you're genuinely curious about them and want to understand if you can help them. (Remember: you're not supposed to win every instruction!)

What we will teach you with L.A.N.D.S is a heart-centred, emotional approach to selling that will feel so natural and easy to you because it comes from the heart and feels completely authentic. We promise that there are no pushy techniques, no sleazy tactics and no mind-control techniques.

You can honour yourself and your prospects with a powerful sales process that results in a win-win for everyone. It's a process that was taught to us by another one of our mentors, Matt Elwell (who is, in our opinion, the greatest salesperson on the planet). This process has transformed our experience of selling to the point where we have grown to love it. And we never thought we'd say that.

Step 1: LISTEN

The first step, and by far the most important one, is LISTEN. Now, listening is a skill that most people think they're pretty good at. After all, it's just politely waiting until the other person has finished speaking so you can say what you want to say, right? Wrong.

Deep listening to really hear someone and understand them is a superpower and a skill that actually takes a lot of practice. But nail your listening skills, and we promise it will send your conversion rate through the roof. Let go of the pressure to memorise a sales pitch. Instead, focus on honing your listening skills until your prospect trusts you so completely, they won't turn to anyone else to sell their house.

Some of the most powerful conversations and successful outcomes we've had have been when we felt like we hardly spoke a word during the home consultation, and the client has said to us, "I felt like you really understood me." Wow!

Looking back, we've just been genuinely curious, eager to spot an opportunity to help and able to step back and give the prospect the space to talk.

Why are you listening first? Well, you're seeking to achieve a deep understanding of your prospect, not just about their house and their moving plans, but about them as people. What drives them? What motivates them? What do they lie awake at 3 am worrying about?

Selling a home is deeply personal, and as agents, we need to put emotions and heart at the forefront of our selling process. It's why we personally believe that women tend to make exceptionally good estate agents: Soft skills are their superpower.

You're also qualifying them at this point. You need to be absolutely sure that the conversation you are having with them is relevant to them and that you could possibly help them with the outcome they are seeking. You're making sure they absolutely need what you do. Don't be tempted to skip past this bit. It's likely to be the most powerful part of the consultation.

Step 2: ASK

The next step is ASK. You're asking powerful questions to establish whether you and your prospect might be a good fit to work together.

Let go of the need to tell your prospect about all the reasons you should work together, and instead focus on asking some powerful questions that will help you both decide if you're a good fit.

So, how does it work? Well, if you've ever been on any sort of traditional sales training before, you've probably been taught to run through the "features and benefits" of working with you. You may even have been told to create a "Listing Presentation" of slides in a folder (so that's what those estate agent folders are that they all carry around!) or on PowerPoint. You're supposed to sit down with your client and run through the entire presentation, telling them all the things you do and rattling off all the reasons why they should work with you and all the reasons why you're so successful.

But as Matt Elwell says, "When you're telling, you are losing." Great selling is about asking powerful questions. Here are some to start you off:

"What was it that made you call me here today, specifically?"

"What have you seen or heard about my service that might possibly help you?"

"What questions do you have about how working with me could help you get a better result?"

Again, in the words of Matt Elwell, "Telling is hard selling. Asking is powerful selling."

Step 3: NEEDS

The third step in LANDS is to establish the prospect's NEEDS. Do they actually need the service you can provide? Hopefully, if you've spent the time listening and asking great questions, it should be clear by this point what their specific needs are.

If you've done a great job of listening to your prospects and asking some great questions, then you'll have a pretty good idea of their needs at this point. Now is the time for you to repeat those needs back to the prospect in their own words. This does two things: It clarifies to your prospect that you have understood them (whilst giving them the opportunity to correct anything you've misunderstood) and also cements in the prospect's mind(s) all the reasons why they've decided to move.

Based on what the prospect has told you so far, the Needs part of the conversation is a deep dive into their pain points, providing an opportunity to establish how their current situation is negatively affecting them and the urgency with which they need to change the status quo.

For example, your prospect may have told you at the beginning of your meeting that they are hoping to downsize. By a process of great questioning, you'll be establishing in your mind (and theirs) the deep need behind this desire to downsize. They might have grown-up children who they want to help buy a house of their own and need to release equity from their home. They may have a grandchild on the way and need to sell to move closer to their children. They may have urgent health needs, which means they can no longer manage a large garden.

What you're trying to establish here is the real need behind their desire to move. What's causing them pain or discomfort? And then the urgency they feel about getting out of their current situation. How much longer can they remain unsold on the market with their current agent? How long can they continue to pay a gardener to maintain their grounds, etc.

What do they need from you to solve their problem?

The first part of this process (from L to N) should occupy the majority of your time spent with your prospect during the initial home consultation. This might feel strange at first, especially as you might be used to getting on with the home tour as quickly as possible.

However, high-level sales are all about the relationship. We're moving from a transactional relationship to one that requires a high level of trust between you and your client. For this reason, spending time really getting to know your potential customer is critical to establishing trust. It's also essential if they're going to decide that you're the only agent they want to work with to sell their high-value home.

We can sometimes spend up to an hour in the first part of the home consultation, getting to know our prospect, asking powerful questions and getting super clear on their needs. When the time comes for the show round, your prospect might even make a joke like, "Oh my goodness, we haven't even shown you the house yet!"

Step 4: DEMONSTRATE

Now it's time to DEMONSTRATE. Here's a golden rule for this process to work effectively: Do not do any "telling" before you've had the show around the house. If you are showing them your marketing brochures or telling your prospect how you would photograph the house or what you would price it at before this point, you need to step back into "discovery" mode again.

The beauty of this process is that when you've asked great questions in the first part of your meeting, you can refer back to them during the show round, demonstrating your level of understanding. You can highlight aspects of their home that they have told you are no longer working for them, such as a lack of bedrooms or outside space that's too big or too small. You can start to paint a picture in their minds about what their future looks like in their new home. It's powerful stuff.

At this point, rather than reeling off a generic sales script that tells them all about your agency and how many homes you've sold, you can tailor the Demonstrate part of the meeting to show them that you have really understood their goals, desires and challenges and presented a solution so specific and tailored to them that working with you is the only logical choice. Remember that people buy when they feel understood. It's a deeply emotional process that has less to do with logic than you may think. Some agents believe that telling their prospect that they've sold the most homes on that particular road would make them the "logical" choice to work with. And indeed, it would. But this is not how people make buying decisions.

Your job is to make the prospect feel really understood and then present the solution to their challenges in your unique, authentic way. This way, working with you feels like the only decision and everyone else is left out of the race, even those agents who have sold more homes on the street than you!

You can say to your prospect, "The great news is that, based on what you've told me, I believe that our 7 Steps to Sold process (or whatever your unique process is), will put you in the best possible position to sell in the fastest time and for the most money, so you can be closer to your grandchildren/release equity/get your kids into their chosen school. Helping clients like you to sell their homes is exactly what we specialise in."

Then, follow up with, "What information do you need from me so that you can consider working with me?"

At this point in the home consultation, reiterate to the prospect some of the key information they've shared and present the solutions that working with you will bring. For example, if they've been on the market previously and were unhappy with their photographs, you'll want to show them your beautiful property brochures with fantastic high-quality pictures and talk about the power of lifestyle photography. If you offer video tours, this is the moment to wax lyrical about how a video of their home will help it really come to life and stand out against the competition online.

Or, they might comment on the lack of viewing feedback or general communication from their last agent. You will have asked them how they prefer to be communicated with (phone, WhatsApp, email), and now is the opportunity to show them how your weekly communication process, using their preferred method, ensures they are always kept up to date and in control.

See how this works so beautifully? You can completely let go of the need to memorise a standard sales pitch and a list of facts and figures. We're all about making things simple and authentic here at Stowhill Estates, because neither of us likes a sleazy sales process, whether on the giving or receiving end!

If you've struggled before to "pitch" in a home consultation, you'll find this process a lifeline. We're here to tell you that you can release all of that stress and focus on listening, asking great questions, establishing their needs, demonstrating how you can help (only if you genuinely can) and then helping them determine the next steps to working together. It's simple, clear, authentic and empowering.

Step 5: NEXT STEPS

Then, we move on to STEPS. What are the logical next steps to take now that you have *listened* to your prospect and *asked* great questions in order to get a deep understanding of their *needs*? You have *demonstrated* how working with you could be the solution to their problems and how you can help them achieve the results they need.

Now, you need to decide together on the logical next steps. Are you a good match to work together, and could working with you get your prospect the results they need? Or do you need to part company as friends and wish them well with another agent?

If you have followed the process closely up until now, this part should become clear, and it's a straightforward next step to get the contracts signed and start working together. If you've followed this process and you're a great fit for each other, this part should become like a no-brainer.

You know those meetings where the rapport is immediately established, you discuss working together and everything flows smoothly and feels exciting? That's what we're trying to recreate with this process, so you work with more of those types of clients and let go of the ones who are going to make life difficult for you.

It's important to remember, though, that the deal is not done at this point. Many agents do everything perfectly in the first part of the home consultation and then mess it up at this point by either not explaining to the client what the next steps are for working together or failing to secure a follow-up date.

Beware of leaving the process open-ended, or you'll risk being ghosted on email and phone, wondering what you did wrong, whilst another agent (who is better at closing!) swoops in and gets the contract signed. This has happened to us so many times, and it's painful.

A top tip is to text or WhatsApp the client within ten minutes of the home consultation ending, expressing how much you enjoyed meeting them, confirming you'll be sending over the proposal within the next 24 hours and reiterating the dates you've agreed to follow up.

You must ensure that, before ending the meeting, you have both agreed on what the next steps will be. Ideally, they will make a decision there and then to work with you, but more often than not, they will need a day or two to consider it, and you will need to follow up with a written proposal. Speed is of the essence here. One of Michael's favourite sayings is, "Time kills deals." It's on you to keep the excitement levels high and the deal moving forward.

You're leaving the home consultation on an emotional high, excited and eager to work together. Then you kill the momentum by taking three days to follow up with your proposal. Don't let this be you! Your written proposal should be sent to your prospect, ideally the same day, or if that's not possible, then certainly within 24 hours. You've already agreed on timescales to follow up at the end of your in-person meeting, so they'll be expecting your call so they can ask any final questions before signing your contract.

It's super important that you are crystal clear about exactly what happens next when a prospect decides to work with you. You'll be amazed at how many agents don't have a clear, step-by-step onboarding process. Remember that your prospect is looking for certainty, clarity and transparency from you. Make it easy for them to work with you!

No Pitch, No Pressure, Just Results

And there you have it: no slick pitch, no PowerPoint presentation, no performing like it's the estate agency edition of *Britain's Got Talent*.

Just a simple, powerful framework that lets you stop chasing clients like a lovesick teenager and start attracting them like a seasoned pro who actually knows their worth (because you do).

When you lead with listening, ask the right questions and show up like a calm, confident human instead of a desperate agent with a valuation gun, magic happens. People lean in. They open up. And then...they say "yes."

When you stop performing and start connecting, when you swap assumptions for curiosity and when you let your prospect feel truly seen and understood, something magical happens.

You stop chasing. You start attracting.

You stop pitching. You start partnering.

You stop trying to "win" the client, and instead, you earn their trust.

So go forth and LAND those listings. Use this process, tweak it and make it your own. Because once you master this, you won't just win more instructions, you'll win the *right* ones. The ones who don't haggle over fees, ghost your follow-ups or call you "the girl from the agency" even after three months of working together.

This is where the fun begins. This is where selling gets easy. This is how you build the business (and life) you actually want.

Now, go out there and let those listings land right in your lap – gracefully, effortlessly and maybe even with a celebratory G&T in hand.

Chapter 8
Luxury Never Goes on Sale

How to Position, Price and Protect Your Value in the High-Stakes World of Premium Property Sales

If you're still squirming when it comes to talking about your fees, you're not alone – but it's costing you. It's costing you time, energy, confidence and quite possibly the very clients who would happily pay more, if only you believed you were worth it.

Most estate agents are undercharging and over-delivering. They're afraid to ask for a higher fee or an upfront payment because they think they need to "earn the right" first. They stay polite, people-pleasing and overly accommodating in the hope that being nice will secure the instruction. But in the high-value homes space, niceness won't win you the business. Leadership will.

Clients selling premium homes don't want the cheapest agent. They want the *right* agent. The one who shows up with clarity, confidence and a plan. And here's the thing: if you can't communicate your value, you're already losing. Because the most successful agents in this space aren't necessarily the most experienced. The experts are the ones who've mastered how to position themselves as experts, guide the conversation and never apologise for their fee.

You're not selling your time. You're not selling a transaction. You're selling a result. A carefully negotiated deal. A seamless process. A beautifully marketed home that commands attention and achieves a premium price. And that's worth something. In fact, it's worth a lot.

This chapter is going to help you:

- Charge what you're truly worth (and feel good about it)
- Justify your fees with confidence, not defensiveness
- Structure your services in a way that clients can clearly see the value
- Introduce upfront payments as a natural and logical part of your offering
- Handle objections gracefully—and close the deal on your terms

When you learn how to confidently lead these conversations, everything changes. Your clients respect you more. Your marketing improves. Your results improve. And – spoiler alert – so does your income.

Ready to stop selling yourself short? Let's go.

You're Not Selling a Commodity

You're not a product on a shelf. You're a trusted advisor, and it's time to act like one.

One of the biggest reasons estate agents struggle to charge higher fees or introduce upfront payments is because, deep down, they're seeing themselves as just another agent. A service provider. A box-ticker in a crowded market. And when you see yourself that way, you unconsciously price yourself that way too: low, apologetically and in constant fear of being undercut.

But here's the truth: You are not a commodity. You are not interchangeable. You are not selling square footage or the number of bedrooms. You are selling expertise. Strategy. Confidence. Clarity. Results. You are the difference between a stressful sale and a seamless one. Between underselling and breaking a street record. That's not something you can get from an online agency or from the "cheapest fee on the high street."

In the high-value homes market, you're not just a facilitator; you're a trusted advisor. And premium clients don't want the cheapest. They want the best. They want to work with someone who understands the emotional, financial and reputational stakes of their sale, and who knows how to lead the process with authority, not just react to it.

This mindset shift is where it all begins.

When you start seeing yourself as a value creator, rather than a cost, everything changes.

You stop comparing yourself to other agents and start articulating what sets you apart.

You stop fearing objections and start welcoming them as opportunities to demonstrate your value.

You stop apologising for your fee and start owning it with clarity and conviction.

Before we discuss strategy, let's be clear: Securing higher fees isn't about being arrogant, pushy, or overpriced. It's about finally recognising what you actually deliver, and having the courage to stand behind it.

And besides, have you ever noticed that the clients who try and beat you down on your fee at the start are always the ones who are a nightmare to work with all the way through?

Your next instruction won't be won by trying to be liked. It will be won by showing up as a leader.

Creating Perceived Value Before the Fee Conversation

The best fee conversations are won before they even begin.

Here's something most agents never realise: By the time you get to the "what's your fee?" moment, the decision has already been made. Either the client sees you as worth it, or they don't. Either they trust you to lead, or they're still deciding whether to trust you at all.

This is why securing higher fees (and upfront payments) starts long before you talk about numbers. It starts with perception. With the way you show up, how you communicate, what you say and, crucially, what you demonstrate before the client even asks about the price.

Perceived Value Starts the Moment They First Encounter You

Your website. Your social media. The brochure you send. Your valuation visit. Every single touchpoint is an opportunity to say, "I'm not like the others." If your content feels templated, if your language is generic, if your brand says "standard," you're telling them your fee should be standard, too.

But if everything they see and feel is elevated, beautiful, thoughtful, professional, *different* – you've already started to anchor a premium perception. You're not just offering estate agency services. You're offering an experience. And clients will always pay more for an experience that makes them feel safe, supported and well-served.

Authority First, Fees Second

Before discussing fees, you must first establish authority. That means:

- Clearly outline your process (so they see the logic and structure behind your service)

- Demonstrating your market knowledge (so they trust your pricing and strategy)

- Asking insightful, confident questions that show you understand both their property and their priorities

- Sharing examples of success stories that reflect *their* situation

All of this creates trust. And trust is the foundation of value.

Package Your Service Like a Product

If you're still listing everything you "do" in a bulleted list (Rightmove listing, photos, floorplans, etc.), you're selling a commodity. Instead, name your process. Give it shape. Call it something. Create tiers or packages if you want to offer options, but never let them reduce your service to a list of tasks.

For example:

"We call it our 7 Steps to Sold Process: It's our signature approach to marketing unique homes in a way that commands maximum attention and price. It includes full styling, cinematic video, targeted social media and a personalised PR strategy."

Suddenly, you're not just another agent offering photos and Rightmove. You're offering a premium launch experience. One that justifies a premium fee.

In short, perceived value drives actual fees. The more effectively you communicate your value before the money talks, the less likely you are to face objections and the more likely you are to be paid what you're worth.

How to Justify Higher Fees Without Defensiveness

One of the biggest mistakes agents make when discussing fees is slipping into defensiveness. They justify. They apologise. They explain at length why they're "worth it" and, in doing so, unintentionally create doubt where there wasn't any before.

Premium agents don't justify. They stand in their value.

You don't have to "sell" your fee if you've already shown the client the quality of your service, the clarity of your process and the confidence of your leadership. By the time you talk about the investment, it should feel like a natural next step, not an awkward negotiation.

Here's how you stay confident – and avoid defensiveness – when it comes to discussing fees:

Lead the Fee Conversation, Don't Wait to Be Asked

Confident agents don't tiptoe around fees or hope the client won't notice. They address it early and elegantly as part of outlining the strategy.

For example:

"This is how we would position and market your home for the best result. To deliver this level of service, our fee is 2%

inclusive of VAT, with a payment on account of £1,800 due on contract signature. I'll walk you through exactly what that includes."

Simple. Clear. Unapologetic.

Sell Outcomes, Not Activities

Remember: No client actually cares about how many brochures you print or whether you post on social media twice or five times a week. What they care about is the result. Higher sale price. Shorter time on the market. Smoother experience.

When discussing your fee, focus on the outcome:

"Our bespoke marketing strategy is designed to maximise competitive tension and achieve the highest possible price."

"Our negotiation expertise regularly adds 5% to 10% to the final selling price, which more than covers our fee."

"Our average sale price is 104% of the original asking price, so our clients end up with more money at the end of the transaction, even after taking our fee into account."

Use Data and Social Proof

The more you can show rather than tell, the less you have to justify. Show examples of homes you sold above the asking price. Share testimonials from happy sellers who initially questioned the fee and were delighted with the outcome. You can also use stats like, "On average, our listings sell 20% faster and achieve 104% of the asking price compared to the local market average."

Facts remove emotion from the conversation.

Frame Your Fee as an Investment, Not a Cost

Use language that positions your fee as an investment in the result, not a cost to be avoided.

Instead of: "Our fee is 2%, which covers XYZ..."

Try: "To deliver this level of service and maximise your return, the investment is 2%. Here's what that unlocks for you..."

Notice the shift in energy? One feels like an invoice. The other feels like a pathway to a better result.

A key reminder:

You are not asking for permission.

You are offering a premium service. You are inviting them to invest in a better outcome.

You are standing in your values. When you do that, your best clients will gladly stand with you.

Structuring Your Offer for Maximum Confidence

One of the best ways to command higher fees and secure upfront payments is to package your service like a premium product, not a collection of tasks. People don't pay luxury prices for a long to-do list. They pay for clarity, certainty and a clearly defined outcome.

When you structure your offer with confidence and precision, you eliminate confusion, create desirability and make your premium fee feel like the obvious, logical investment it is.

Here's how to do it.

Give Your Process a Name

When you name your process, you immediately make it feel unique, proprietary, and valuable.

Instead of: "We take photos, write a listing and put you on Rightmove..."

Say:

"We use our Signature 7 Steps to Sold System, designed specifically for unique and high-value homes. It includes strategic pricing, lifestyle-driven staging, cinematic video storytelling and a targeted social media launch to maximise buyer competition and achieve the best possible price."

Naming your system makes it sound like something they can only get from you.

Break It Into Stages (And Attach Value to Each Stage)

Rather than presenting a one-line "start to finish" service, break your process into phases and explain the value of each one.

For example:

Preparation Phase: Home styling consultation, property audit, bespoke marketing strategy

Launch Phase: Professional photography, cinematic video, magazine-style brochure creation, PR outreach

Sales Phase: Strategic viewings management, negotiation expertise, proactive chain progression

Each phase feels deliberate, considered and essential. It feels *premium*.

Build In an Upfront Investment

Position your upfront fee as a natural part of launching a high-value home professionally.

For example:

"To get things started with our 7 Steps to Sold Process, we require a payment on account of investment of £1,800, which enables us to confirm the professional photography, cinematic videography, targeted online campaigns and a custom-designed property brochure. This upfront investment ensures your home receives the world-class presentation it deserves."

By presenting it early, naturally and as an essential part of achieving the best price, you eliminate the feeling that you're "asking for extra." Instead, you're leading with professionalism.

Offer Options, But Keep Them Premium

If you want to provide choice, offer 2–3 elevated packages, and never a "cheap" version.

For example:

Signature Launch: Our full-service bespoke marketing package

Prestige Plus: Includes everything in Signature Launch + national PR outreach + hosted open house events

Ultimate Elite Launch: Full service plus a cinematic lifestyle film, drone video, custom branding for the home (property logo, branded signage), and a dedicated social media ad campaign

This allows clients to choose how much premium they want, not whether they want a premium at all.

Position It This Way

"Our goal is to create maximum buyer desire and achieve the best price possible for your home. To achieve this, we invest in a full, bespoke launch strategy. Here's how we deliver it and what it unlocks for you."

When you structure your offer with confidence, it no longer feels like you're trying to "justify" your fee. You're simply presenting a premium experience and inviting the client to step into it.

How to Introduce and Secure Upfront Payments

Professional agents get paid upfront because they're not just taking photos; they're launching a product.

If you've ever felt uncomfortable asking for an upfront payment, you're not alone. Many agents worry it'll scare clients off, make them seem too pushy or put them at a disadvantage compared to agents who work on a "no sale, no fee" model.

But here's the truth: In a premium agency, requesting an upfront marketing fee doesn't undermine your professionalism. Rather, it proves it.

Premium clients don't want the cheapest; they want the best. And when you ask for a commitment upfront, you're showing them you take their home (and your service) seriously. You're not just throwing it up on Rightmove and hoping for the best. You're making an investment in their result and asking them to do the same.

Here's how to introduce it confidently and naturally.

Make It a Standard Part of Your Process

If you present an upfront payment like it's negotiable or unusual, clients will pick up on that hesitation. Instead, present it in a standard and professional manner.

"As part of our 7 Steps to Sold process, we ask for a £1,800 marketing investment up front. This covers all styling guidance, professional photography, cinematic video, a luxury brochure and your personalised digital campaign."

Say it like you've said it a hundred times before – because soon, you will.

Link It to Tangible Deliverables

Clients are happy to invest if they understand what they're getting. Don't just say "marketing." Instead, spell out what they'll receive.

"This includes a two-hour styling session, architectural photography, drone footage, a custom-designed brochure and targeted social media promotion. It's the foundation of a powerful launch, and it's what allows us to consistently outperform the local market."

Position It as a Commitment, Not a Fee

Words matter. Don't call it a charge, call it an investment. And explain how it benefits them.

"This small investment also helps ensure mutual commitment. It means we're both committed to achieving the best possible outcome for you. We only take on a handful of clients at any one time, so we want to give your home the full focus and attention it deserves."

Premium clients respect this. It actually builds trust.

Show Social Proof That Others Happily Pay It

If you're still building your confidence, social proof helps enormously.

"Every client we've worked with in the past two years has made this same investment, and they'll tell you it was worth every penny. In fact, many say it's what helped them fall back in love with their home before selling."

Include It in Your Agreement, Up Front

Don't bury it in the small print. Include it in your proposal, discuss it during your pitch and have a clear, signed agreement with payment terms. You'll find that when you act like it's normal, it becomes normal.

If They Push Back...

You don't need to go into defensive mode. Keep it light, warm and grounded in your standards.

"I completely understand, and I know this isn't something every agent does. But we're not like every agent. Our clients choose us for a reason, and this process is part of what helps us deliver above-average results. If it's important to you to minimise upfront cost, we may not be the right fit – and that's okay."

Powerful. Polite. Professional.

A professional service deserves professional commitment.

When you introduce upfront payments with clarity, conviction and calm, you won't just secure better listings; you'll secure better clients.

Negotiation Techniques to Protect Your Fee

You've delivered a brilliant pitch. The client nods. They love your marketing, your style, your approach. And then... it happens:

"We love what you do. However, another agent said they would do it for 1%. Can you match that?"

This is the moment where many agents go weak at the knees. And it's the moment where the *elite* agents rise.

What you do next doesn't just determine your fee; it determines your positioning, credibility and power.

Discounting your fee undermines everything you've just said about your value. And here's the kicker: Even if the client agrees to work with you, they'll always question your confidence. "If they gave way on price that quickly, what else will they compromise on?"

Here's how to hold your ground with confidence and composure.

Don't Flinch. Breathe.

First, resist the urge to fill the silence or go straight into defence mode. Stay calm. Smile.

"I understand. Would it be helpful if I explained how our fee is structured and what it includes?"

You're not thrown. You're in control. And that matters more than you think.

Reframe the Conversation Around Value

Bring it back to outcomes, not cost.

"The agents charging 1% usually take on a much higher volume of homes and need to sell quickly to meet their numbers. Our model is different. We work with a small number of clients, allowing us to deliver the kind of personalised, premium service that yields better results. That's what our clients are paying for, and why we consistently achieve above-market prices."

This is the difference between price and worth.

Use "Give-Get" if You Need Wiggle Room

If you do need to offer some flexibility (though it should be rare), create a trade, not a discount.

"We can reduce our fee slightly, but we'd remove the drone video and limit the social media campaign. Those elements make a huge impact, so if it's important to keep them, I'd recommend staying with our full package."

This keeps you in the driver's seat and demonstrates to the client that value and price are closely linked.

Mirror Their Concern and Lean into Confidence

Sometimes, the best tactic is to calmly hold your position while reinforcing your professionalism.

"I completely understand wanting to compare fees, as it's an important decision. What I've found is that our clients are often initially tempted by a cheaper option, but ultimately choose us because they know we'll achieve the best result and make the process feel seamless. And that peace of mind? It's worth far more than 0.5%."

Be Willing to Walk Away (Respectfully)

One of the most powerful tools you have is the willingness to say no.

"We may not be the cheapest, and we're never going to try to be. If price is your top priority, there are plenty of agents who will meet that brief. But if you want a result that reflects the true value of your home, and an experience that makes the process enjoyable, not stressful – I'd love to work with you."

And here's the magic: Often, that's the moment they decide to go with you.

Remember this:

You are not just selling a service. You are selling leadership. Confidence. Results.

The moment you discount your fee without hesitation, you discount your value in their eyes.

Stand firm. Speak with clarity. And let your confidence be contagious.

Handling Objections Like a Pro

When a client raises an objection about your fee or upfront payment, it's easy to feel defensive. But most of the time, they're not trying to knock you down; they're trying to understand whether the investment is worth it. They're weighing risk, trying to make a smart decision and looking to see how you handle pressure.

And that's your cue to lead.

Because great agents don't avoid objections, they welcome them. They view objections as opportunities to reinforce value, build trust, and take control of the conversation.

Here are some of the most common objections, and how to handle them with calm confidence:

Objection #1: "Another agent will do it for less."

What they're really saying: "Help me understand why you're worth more."

Your response:

"Absolutely, they will. But they're also likely working with 30+ properties at once, meaning limited attention, rushed marketing and a higher risk of underselling your home. We only work with a small number of clients at a time, which means you get our full focus and the kind of bespoke marketing and skilled negotiation that consistently delivers above-market results. It's not about being the cheapest. It's about being the most effective."

Objection #2: "I don't want to pay anything upfront."

What they're really saying: "I'm not sure I trust that I'll get what I pay for."

Your response:

"I completely understand. What we've found is that when both parties are committed from the start, the results are consistently better. This upfront investment allows us to put serious energy and resources behind the launch of your home, from styling and video to print materials and targeted online campaigns. It's not just a listing, it's a full-scale, story-led marketing campaign designed to attract the right buyers and secure the best price."

Objection #3: "That's more than I was expecting."

What they're really saying: "You're more expensive than I budgeted – convince me it's worth it."

Your response:

"Totally fair. We're not the cheapest option – and we never try to be. Our clients don't choose us based on our fees; they choose us because we consistently deliver stronger results, less stress, and a more enjoyable experience. And in this market, a smoother process and a stronger sale price often means that we more than pay for ourselves."

Objection #4: "Can you match what the other agent offered us?"

What they're really saying: "Let's see how confident you really are in your fee."

Your response:

"We get that question a lot. But our model isn't built on matching others, it's built on maximising results. The reason we achieve what we do is because we invest more energy, time and creativity into every instruction. We've found that when we adhere to our process and pricing, it yields the best possible outcome for our clients. I'd love to deliver that result for you too."

Bonus Tip: Don't Argue. Align.

Never get combative or defensive. Instead, align with their concern and lead them to clarity.

"I completely understand, it's a big decision. That's why we put so much care into getting it right, from day one. If you'd like to speak with some of our past clients, I'd be happy to connect you with them. They'll tell you exactly what their experience was like."

Objections are simply moments of hesitation. Handle them with grace, and you'll often turn a "maybe" into a resounding "yes."

Closing the Conversation with Certainty

You've walked the property. You've delivered your pitch. You've outlined your strategy, presented your fee and handled their questions with clarity and calm. Now comes the part where many agents wobble: Closing the conversation.

If you've led the discussion well, closing should feel effortless. In fact, the more confidently and naturally you close, the more confident the client will feel saying "yes." Your energy will become their reassurance.

Be Clear and Decisive

Clients don't want vague language. They want leadership. So don't ask:

"Would you like to go ahead?"

Instead, assume they do, and lead with clarity:

"Shall we book your media day for next Thursday?"

"I'll send over the marketing agreement this afternoon so we can get started."

This project conveys confidence and momentum, making it easy for them to say "yes."

Recap the Value (Not the Fee)

As you close, bring the focus back to the result, not the cost.

"We're really excited to present your home the way it deserves to be seen. With the bespoke marketing we've outlined, our aim is to attract maximum interest, create competitive tension and secure you the very best price."

This reaffirms why they chose you in the first place.

Handle Last-Minute Doubts Gracefully

If the client stalls or asks for time to think, don't panic. Gently keep control of the timeline.

"Of course, this is a big decision. Would it help if I followed up with you tomorrow afternoon?

That way, we can keep momentum and still aim for a launch next week."

Maintain a positive and proactive energy, rather than a desperate or pushy one.

Know When to Stop Talking

One of the most common mistakes agents make is over-explaining right at the finish line. You don't need to re-justify your fee or re-pitch your service. Ask for the business, then let the silence do the heavy lifting.

"Shall we get things started?"

Then pause. Let them speak.

Silence isn't uncomfortable. It's powerful.

Close With Certainty, Leave With Momentum

You want your client walking away thinking, "Yes, this was the right decision. I'm in safe hands." That feeling comes from how you carry yourself in the final minutes. Calm. Confident. Professional. Warm. Like someone who's done this a hundred times, and is going to handle it all beautifully.

In the end, closing the deal isn't about pressure. It's about presence. The more you believe in your value, the more your client will, too.

Higher Fees Are Earned Through Energy, Not Just Experience

There's a myth in this industry that you have to wait years – decades even – before you can charge what you're truly worth. That the right to higher fees comes with grey hair and a long list of sales, but that's not how a premium agency works.

The truth? Higher fees are earned through energy, not just experience.

Through the way you show up, the clarity of your offer, the confidence in your voice and the leadership you provide from the very first conversation.

Yes, expertise matters. But what sets elite agents apart isn't just how many homes they've sold, it's how powerfully they position themselves, how professionally they package their service and how unapologetically they ask for what they're worth.

This chapter wasn't just about pricing. It was about permission.

Permission to stop undercharging.

Permission to stop people-pleasing.

Permission to stop blending in with agents who do the bare minimum and race to the bottom.

You're not here to be the cheapest. You're here to be the most valuable. To deliver a client experience so elevated, so considered, so results-focused that the question isn't, "Why are you more expensive?" It's "How soon can we get started?"

So hold your fee. Introduce that upfront investment. And say it all with certainty, not an apology.

Because when you stand in your value, your clients will, too.

Chapter 9
The Power of World-Class Property Marketing

Why Extraordinary Presentation Wins Instructions,
Sells Faster, and Builds Your Brand

When we first started out, we genuinely believed that the best way to stand out in estate agency was through sheer availability. Work harder. Be there 24/7. Answer every call. Clean the client's kitchen if you have to.

Our pitch went something like this: "When you work with Stowhill Estates, you get me and Lucy from start to finish. We work tirelessly with you and will do absolutely everything ourselves. And what's more, you can reach us by phone at any time, including weekends and holidays; we're available to you. Here are our personal mobile numbers."

And while that hustle helped us win hearts early on, it wasn't sustainable. More importantly, it wasn't scalable.

What we realised (after scrubbing one too many toilets!) is that true differentiation in this industry doesn't come from how available you are. It comes from how you present, position and promote the homes you're selling.

It comes from the emotional pull, the story you tell and the experience you create. That's where bespoke, world-class property marketing changes the game. In this chapter, we'll show you how to move from being a helpful agent to being an unforgettable one. The kind of agent who not only achieves better results but who attracts the very best clients simply by showing what's possible.

How We Discovered That Scrubbing Toilets Isn't a Scaling Strategy

We remember one particular home with a client who was a single man. We don't think he'd cleaned his kitchen since his wife left him ten years previously, and his "wardrobe" was a chair in the corner of his bedroom, piled high with dirty t-shirts and pants.

This would have put the majority of "lesser" estate agents off. But oh no, not superheroes Lucy and Michael! Michael donned his rubber gloves and, armed with a bottle of bleach, set about sterilising the kitchen. Whilst Lucy sorted through the huge pile of clothes, hanging up some and putting others in the laundry.

Michael quipped that he used to have a "proper job." The interesting thing is that we thought we were differentiating ourselves, and this is how you become a "full-service" agent. Instead, what we were actually doing was undermining our expertise and authority.

How could the client trust us to negotiate the sale of their million-pound home when we were scrubbing their loo three weeks previously?

The other challenge with being available all the time is that it stunts your growth. There are only so many hours in the day, and if you're doing absolutely everything on every house sale, eventually you'll run out of time to deliver that level of service. You'll reach a ceiling on the number of homes you can serve. Oh, and remember you also have a life outside of work! It's nice to go on holiday now and again and not have to check your email or take work calls. There had to be a better way of standing out from the competition.

It was around this time that we met our friend and mentor, Sam Ashdown, who taught us the secrets to differentiating our agency using experiential, bespoke marketing. It wouldn't be an overstatement to say that it transformed our business by setting us apart from the competition, helped us take on the "big boys" in the corporates and gave us a really distinct selling proposition for the right sort of client.

What Bespoke Property Marketing Really Means

Bespoke property marketing isn't just about slapping a logo on a brochure or using a fancy font. Rather, it's a completely tailored strategy designed around a single, specific home. It's about creating a one-of-a-kind marketing campaign that captures the essence of the property and speaks directly to the type of buyer who will fall in love with it.

That might mean hand-styling each room for the photo shoot, crafting emotive, story-driven copy, designing a magazine-style brochure, creating cinematic video tours or launching a social media and PR campaign to attract buyers well beyond the portals.

What it's not is generic template brochures, one-size-fits-all descriptions or copy-and-paste marketing packages. True bespoke marketing elevates a property's status, maximises its exposure and reflects the level of care, quality and creativity that justifies a premium price – and a premium agent.

Why Premium Agents Must Embrace Bespoke Marketing

Bespoke property marketing is one of the fastest, most effective ways to differentiate yourself in a crowded estate agency market. It's not just about selling homes; it's a powerful marketing tool that attracts the right kind of clients: those who appreciate quality, attention to detail and the care you put into every listing. When prospective sellers see what you do and how beautifully you do it, they'll be naturally drawn to work with you.

If you're positioning yourself as a premium estate agent, your marketing has to walk the talk. Bespoke property marketing is not just a tool to sell homes, it's a statement of your standards, your creativity and your commitment to excellence.

In the high-value homes market, generic simply doesn't cut it. Your clients expect elevated service, attention to detail and results that reflect the calibre of their property. By using bespoke marketing – crafted brochures, cinematic video, tailored social campaigns, story-led copy – you demonstrate that you don't just list homes, you *launch* them.

It sets you apart from the cookie-cutter competition, builds trust with discerning clients and reinforces your personal brand as the go-to agent for high-end, high-care, high-impact results. In a market where perception is everything, bespoke marketing is your competitive edge.

Your valuation conversations become easier, your conversions in the living room increase, and fee objections? Often, they disappear entirely. Why? Because the perceived value of bespoke marketing is so high, it sets you apart from the templated, transactional approach most agents offer.

Instead of trying to compete on vague "service levels," you're offering something truly unique and something very few others are doing. It helps achieve a higher price for the property, builds instant credibility and is, quite honestly, a lot of fun. Crafting beautiful brochures, capturing stunning visuals and telling the story of a home in a way that makes your clients beam with pride? That's the kind of work that turns happy clients into raving fans and you into the go-to agent in your area.

Why Corporates Can't Do Bespoke

When you move into the high-value homes market, every home you sell will be unique, with its own stand-alone appealing qualities, features and quirks. Your job as the agent is to highlight these features and tease out the very best elements of the property, showcasing them in the most compelling way. There's no doubt about it, bespoke marketing will truly set you apart.

Twenty years ago, the likes of Savills, Knight Frank and Hamptons were the "go-to" agencies for high-end homes. If you had a million-pound-plus home, these sorts of posh but frankly rather stuffy agencies were your only choice. You'd call in the agent, probably with a double-barrelled surname (we call them the "red trouser brigade"), they'd take some pictures, put an ad in Country Life and the Telegraph and call around their circle of well-connected friends and acquaintances to search for a potential buyer.

The advent of the internet and sites like Rightmove and OnTheMarket have changed all that. Agents complain about the cost of Rightmove, but the truth is, it has levelled the playing field completely, meaning that we can all access high-net-worth buyers and sellers. They are no longer contained within the little black book of Hugo Huntingdon-Smythe at Savills. And besides, have you seen the cost of print advertising lately? It makes Rightmove seem cheap in comparison.

The democratisation of home selling through the internet and property portals means that agents have had to become skilled marketers and learn how to present homes at their best online. It's no longer good enough for the agent to pop round with a digital camera. And here's the truth, which might annoy you: The vast majority of estate agents are not good at marketing (themselves *or* properties!) and therein lies your golden opportunity.

The challenge with most corporate agents is that, due to their sheer size and the volume of transactions they handle, they often have to take a cookie-cutter, one-size-fits-all approach to their property marketing. This means that every home will get the same number of photos, the same boilerplate-type description and the same templated brochure, leaving no room for the unique lifestyle aspects that make a house truly a home.

This is where you come in and can blow them away with bespoke marketing. By taking the approach that every new home you list is an individual, stand-alone marketing project, you can start to decide who the type of ideal buyer is likely to be for that home and then start to craft the individual, bespoke elements about the house that make it most appealing to that ideal buyer.

Consider who is most likely to buy this home and how to best appeal to them. Then, you can decide which specific channels you can use to reach them most effectively.

Let's explore how to deliver world-class property marketing that will help you stand out against the competition and attract your ideal client to you.

Before you read on, we have two caveats: Firstly, you need to keep an open mind. World-class property marketing simply cannot be done on a tight budget. You will need to accept that it will cost you more to deliver this kind of marketing. A lot more. You need to be prepared to invest in yourself at the beginning if you want to achieve the results at the end. To paraphrase the old saying, "You can't deliver champagne with a beer budget."

Secondly, you need to trust the process. We're going to suggest you do things that go against everything you might have been taught. We're going to suggest you say "no" to the wrong types of homes (yes, potentially leaving money on the table). You're going to want to cut corners and try to find someone who can do it "cheaper." And you're going to want to do some (or all) of it yourself. We know this because we've been there. We've bought the swanky digital camera, thinking we can do the photos ourselves. We've hired Lucy's dad and his drone to do the aerial shots, and we've used ChatGPT to write the property descriptions.

Here's what we know: You can't expect to deliver the sort of marketing that blows your clients away on the cheap. You have to be prepared to put your money where your mouth is.

You're going to tell us that you can't afford it and that it won't work in your area. But we're going to challenge you and tell you that in order for this to work, you have to put your fees up and charge an up-front fee because it's what your clients want.

If you don't believe us, then think about some of the top luxury brands. Do they ever go on sale? Would you ever walk into the Ferrari dealership and ask what deals they have on? Do you ever see those giant red "50% off everything" posters in the windows of Prada and Louis Vuitton? To truly differentiate yourself, you must adopt this same mindset. Remember the lesson from Chapter 8? Quality never goes on sale.

If you start offering this amazing marketing at a 1% fee, your clients will smell a rat. Here's the beauty of this: They *expect* you to be expensive, and they already know you are going to cost more than the agent down the road because they will have seen the quality of your marketing. And they don't care! The clients that are attracted to you want *you*. In fact, sometimes it can be a relief when we tell them we are "only 1.5% or only 2%"!

It can take some time to get your head around this, but we promise you the mindset shift will help you attract and convert exactly the right clients for you, and, just as importantly, weed out the time-wasters that are after a discount service and wouldn't pay your fee anyway. Let them go to Purplebricks – just let them go. They are not your clients, and that's okay.

You must accept that poorly executed or cost-effective property marketing is more damaging to your brand than not marketing at all. And we've seen some terrible property marketing over the years!

However, we promise that if you follow the process correctly, a modest investment will yield multiple dividends, resulting in higher sales prices for your sellers and a steady stream of potential clients coming your way, as they love what you do and want it for themselves.

Here are the key elements of a bespoke property marketing campaign.

Key Element # 1: Home Styling

In today's competitive property market, first impressions are crucial. Buyers often decide within seconds whether a home feels right, and home styling or staging can transform a property into an inviting space that appeals to a broad audience, facilitating quicker sales and potentially higher offers.

After photography, your ability to style and present a home in the most compelling way will be the key to helping you stand out as a high-end agent. Home styling is one of the areas of property marketing where you can have the greatest impact, particularly if the home has been previously listed for sale with another agent. We often hear from our clients that once we have worked our magic with home styling and fresh photography, their home looks like a completely different property.

Buyers process visual information rapidly and subconsciously, so a well-styled home allows them to envision their lives within the space, creating an emotional connection that can drive purchasing decisions. Conversely, cluttered or overly personalised spaces may hinder this connection, making it harder for buyers to see the home's true potential.

And the figures back this up:

Faster Sales: Staged homes sell up to 73% faster than non-staged ones.

Higher Offers: Staged properties can command 5-15% more than their un-staged counterparts.

Increased Viewings: An enhanced presentation leads to more online clicks and in-person viewings, thereby broadening the pool of potential buyers.

Home styling can also be a highly effective way of gaining trust and loyalty from your clients, but it's important to approach it sensitively and always keep the client's feelings at the top of mind. Remember, they are letting you into their most personal and private space, and you are being entrusted with selling what is likely to be their biggest financial asset. So, diplomacy, empathy and sensitivity in your approach to styling their home for sale are crucial.

You are not there to criticise their level of housekeeping or their taste in interior furnishings. Your job is to gently guide them to understanding that the way you sell a home is very different from the way you live in one, and that by following your expertise, they will ultimately achieve a smoother sale with a higher price.

Remember, not everyone will "get" it, especially if your client is more of a left-brained, analytical thinker rather than a creative type. And no matter how large the value of the home, some people are just plain messy!

Occasionally, we've had potential clients tell us they "don't want the flowers and croissants stuff." They just don't get it, and that's okay (actually, it's on us because it means we haven't done a good enough job of educating our prospects as to why it's beneficial). However, if they truly don't understand or aren't interested, that's fine. They're not our client, and we kindly release them to work with another agent who has a more transactional, less bespoke approach. Thankfully, this situation is becoming rare, as we tend to only attract clients who want to work with us *because* of the croissants and flowers!

Ultimately, the reason for investing time and effort into home styling for the client is to present their home to the market in the most appealing way possible, thereby attracting the most online clicks, viewings and ultimately, the highest offers.

The reason you, as an agent, should embrace home styling is so that you elicit loyalty and confidence from your clients and potential clients by demonstrating that you implicitly understand how to market and present a unique home in the most compelling way. It also leads to great photos of amazingly presented homes that you can use over and over again to promote yourself and your agency.

Learning how to style and present a home for sale is relatively simple and easy to learn. It also doesn't have to be expensive. There are a few key tips and tricks that are simple and effective and can be learned quickly by you and your team.

Top Tips for Home Styling

Start With Key Accessories

Firstly, home styling is not something you need to outsource. It can be done fairly simply with a bit of training and some key props and accessories. If you're just starting on offering home styling to your clients, it's worth investing in a few key pieces that will have maximum impact and can be reused at every shoot. Then, you can build up your library of accessories as you go. The client will often have items in their home that you can use and repurpose as well. Just remember to ask permission before you go rifling through their kitchen cupboards to find the antique tea set!

There are some great suppliers of styling accessories these days, including old favourites like IKEA, as well as HomeSense,

Home Bargains and even Amazon. With a budget of around £500, you can build a simple portfolio of styling accessories that you can take to every styling shoot.

Begin with versatile items that can be reused across properties, such as neutral cushions and throws, simple artwork, quality bedding (our preference is white) and fresh or faux plants and flowers.

Consult and Communicate

In the early days, we encountered a few setbacks on our styling shoots, primarily due to an over-enthusiastic home stylist on the team and a lack of communication, which left the homeowner feeling uncomfortable and overwhelmed. It's why we now have a pre-media day consultation with our clients, where we explain exactly what will happen on photoshoot day and walk through their homes with them, showing them how we will stage each room.

This secures you crucial buy-in from the client and, importantly, gives the client the opportunity to add their own thoughts as well as let us know if there is anything they definitely don't want to be touched. You can also show the client on this pre-media day exactly how to clear their clutter and remind them to put away items such as toiletries, teddy bears, books, toys, etc. We always provide a couple of large storage boxes for our clients to store their personal items ahead of the photoshoot.

Also, tread carefully. You are looking for opportunities to discuss the best angles for photographs, so you may suggest moving an armchair, for example. You are *not* saying, "Oh my god, those cushions are horrendous and need to go!" If you approach this in the right way, you'll find your clients will be enthusiastic and helpful, and will even add their own suggestions, rather than being defensive and obstructive. If they really don't want something moved or changed, don't force the issue. The aim is to build up trust with your seller, not alienate them or offend them.

Declutter and Depersonalise

One of the kindest and most valuable things you can do for your clients is to gently guide them through the process of decluttering and de-personalising their home before it goes on the market. It's important to help them understand that buyers need to see themselves in the space, not be distracted by someone else's life.

Explain that removing excess furniture, knick-knacks, personal photos and overly bold décor isn't about erasing their personality. Rather, it's about creating a blank canvas that allows buyers to emotionally connect with the home. Encourage them to view it as the first step in moving on, packing away treasured items that they'll soon be unpacking in their next chapter.

Make it easier by offering a checklist or even some practical help on your pre-media day visit. Framing this as a strategic move, rather than a criticism, helps clients feel supported and proud of how beautifully their home presents when it hits the market.

Room-by-Room Strategy

When it comes to home styling, a one-size-fits-all approach simply doesn't work. Every home and every room needs to tell its own part of the story. That's why it's essential to create a clear, room-by-room strategy before media day. Walk through the property in advance and assess each space individually. What is this room's function? What are its strongest features? What needs to be highlighted or downplayed?

In living areas, focus on light, layout and flow. In bedrooms, think calm, neutral and inviting. Kitchens should feel uncluttered and functional, while bathrooms need to be sparkling and inviting, resembling a spa-like environment. Make notes, take photos and list specific styling touches for each space, including any accessories you'll need to bring on the day. This not only ensures a smooth and stress-free photoshoot, but it also helps the home present in its best possible light, literally and figuratively, so it can connect emotionally with potential buyers.

Let Them Get Involved

Yes, it's probably easier if your clients are not around on photoshoot day, but we always invite them to stay and be involved in the action. It's exciting for them to see the buzz around getting their house ready for sale, and it's yet another way for you to differentiate yourself from other agents.

When we arrive with a team of 5 or 6 people, most of our clients are impressed by the time, effort and professionalism that go into creating their property marketing. Media day is also a great opportunity to get to know your clients a little better and build that all-important rapport. Any opportunity you get to build trust and confidence should be embraced.

Leave a Thoughtful Touch

Once the home is beautifully styled and the media day buzz has calmed, leaving behind a small, thoughtful gift is a simple gesture that makes a lasting impression. It could be a bouquet of fresh flowers, a box of artisanal chocolates, a handwritten thank-you card or even a beautifully wrapped candle or a locally sourced treat. It doesn't have to be extravagant; what matters is the intention behind it.

This moment of appreciation tells your client that you value their trust, effort, and collaboration throughout the process. It adds a layer of warmth and professionalism that most agents overlook, subtly reinforcing the premium experience you provide. Little touches like this help turn your clients into raving fans, deepen the relationship and set the tone for a long-term connection built on care, trust and thoughtfulness.

What If You Really Don't Want to Do Home Styling?

If you're not feeling confident about undertaking home styling personally, there's a wealth of professional home staging companies across the UK ready to assist. These experts offer a range of services, from adding finishing touches like cushions, throws and artwork, to providing comprehensive furniture packages for vacant properties.

Their offerings typically include initial consultations, detailed staging plans, furniture and accessory rentals and full installation and styling services. Costs vary based on the property's size and the scope of work, but you can expect to pay anywhere from £250 for a virtual consultation to £10,000 for a full furniture package on a vacant home.

As a general guideline, professional staging costs range from 1% to 2% of the property's asking price. Investing in professional home styling not only enhances your property's market appeal but also often leads to quicker sales and higher offers. For instance, one homeowner invested £11,000 in staging a Georgian house in Somerset, resulting in a sale within three months after previously struggling to sell for six months.

If you're ready to start curating your own portfolio of home styling items, we've created a free handy shopping guide for you. You can download it at <u>www.eliteagentcollective.com/resources</u> or scan the QR code at the end of the book.

Key Element #2: Professional Photography

Photography is by far the most effective way for you and your agency to stand out from the crowd, and therefore it's the most important element of bespoke marketing to get right. Before you move on to any of the other elements of bespoke marketing, make sure you absolutely nail your photography, and you'll already be streets ahead of the competition.

Professional photography is not about taking an online course and buying a fancy digital SLR or the latest iPhone to do the photos yourself! Full disclosure: When we first set up Stowhill Estates, we were absolutely convinced that we could create great images by ourselves, so we went out and spent a few hundred pounds on a high-end camera, only to discover that it was way harder than we had ever imagined.

The camera now sits gathering dust in the office. We haven't used it once in eight years! We much prefer to leave it to the professionals who are adept at creating evocative images and capturing the real essence of a home through the lens.

Not convinced that professional photography is really necessary? Let's share an interesting fact with you. Scientists estimate that humans make 80% of their buying decisions based on emotions and only 20% based on logic. This is why good photography is so powerful in helping a home stand out on Rightmove and enticing the potential buyer to book a viewing.

Good photography is designed to elicit an emotional response. Remember that people choose a home with their heart first. You'll also capture the hearts of your sellers, too! When they see their home looking so wonderful in pictures, they'll remember why they fell in love with it all those years ago, and they'll feel super confident in your ability to sell their home because they know you've really understood their home and everything it offers.

Photo shoot day is a fantastic way to show off your and your team's skills and differentiate yourself from the competition. If your client has been on the market before, they will likely have had photos taken within an hour with a photographer they have never met before, who has been contracted out by their agency.

By contrast, when you turn up with a team of professionals who are there to style and stage the house to make it look incredible, and you're there for most of the day ensuring just the right angles and light, finishing off with a twilight photo session, the difference in service level and therefore perceived value from the client will be palpable. You are already demonstrating why you deserve a higher fee, and the house isn't even on the market yet.

The different types of photography we use are:

Lifestyle Photography

Have you ever looked at property listings online and thought they just looked a bit, well, soul-less? Estate agents often love to declutter rooms, stripping them of their personality along the way, and then take photos from angles and use a fish-eye lens designed to make the room look bigger than it really is. The result is a distorted image that doesn't really capture what it's like to live in that home.

By contrast, lifestyle photography brings the home and all its personality to life on the page or on the screen in front of you. And it's the reason why glossy interior design magazines use this type of imagery all the time. Beautiful, professionally framed and lit photos of a home allow the buyer to imagine themselves living there and attain the lifestyle that is on offer. Which is why it's so powerful at creating an emotional connection with that buyer.

Twilight Imagery

Twilight imagery of the exterior of your home, captured at the perfect time as the sun sets during the Golden Hour, can significantly enhance your online visibility. It's particularly useful in wintertime to make gardens look atmospheric when leaves and plants are sparse and not looking their best.

Getting the twilight shot just right takes real skill and effort. Capturing the sunset during a photoshoot in June will mean being at the home past 10 pm. It can be tempting to consider using AI or Photoshop to just insert a twilight sky into your photos, but despite the amazing technology on offer these days, photoshopped skies almost always look fake.

There's no substitute for the real thing. Plus, when you're standing in your client's garden at 10 pm, they'll be blown away by the time and effort you're putting into marketing their home. Creating that bespoke element is all about doing what other agents can't and won't do, so you can really differentiate yourself.

Aerial Photography

Beyond the bricks and mortar, your buyer is also looking to discover more about the lifestyle that is on offer, so showcasing the local area in your property marketing is essential. A great way to achieve this is through aerial drone photography and video, which works particularly well in rural areas with stunning views or incredible locations.

We've found a huge variation in the quality of drone photographers over the years, so please take some time to do your research (there are many enthusiastic amateur drone photographers out there!). As with most photography, it's a lot harder than it looks!

It generally works better for a larger home if you engage one photographer for both interior and exterior stills, as well as a specialist drone photographer in addition. Drones can be rather sensitive to inclement weather, so your drone photographer may need to conduct more than one visit on different days depending on the conditions.

You may also want to consider engaging them on two visits so they can capture the morning light and twilight, or sunset, for example. Drone photography and videography are a real client-pleaser, too. We've found that our clients love being present when the drone camera takes to the skies and hovers overhead, capturing beautiful footage of their homes and grounds.

A top tip is to engage your drone photographer to capture extra aerial footage of the local area when shooting each home, so you can start to create a library of content and footage for your local area guides and social media content.

Video is an absolute must if you want to maximise the exposure for the homes you're selling. Anecdotally, a property listing with a video receives 403% more enquiries than those without. Plus, video has the added bonus of maximising your exposure as an agent, enabling you to showcase your skills and personality and attract clients to you.

Don't be tempted to do it yourself when you're filming a high-value home. Quick "behind the scenes" and local area videos, as well as property market updates, are fine when filmed on your phone, but when it comes to presenting a luxury home on video, there's no substitute for the professionals!

Luckily, there are now some great companies offering agents professional-quality videos at affordable prices, and many also provide training. Video has literally transformed our business. Not only do we get to channel our inner Phil & Kirsty and show off in front of the camera, but it also gives us huge exposure on Rightmove, YouTube and other social media channels. (Side note, we offer an exclusive one-day video training workshop for ambitious agents four times a year. Get in touch to find out when our next one is!)

A great property video should do more than just walk buyers through the space. It should *invite* them into a lifestyle.

Think of it as a short film, not just a visual floor plan. Start by setting the tone. Is this a calm countryside retreat or a slick city pad? Choose music and pacing that match. Use a mix of sweeping exterior shots, smooth room transitions and close-ups of tactile details, such as a flickering fire, brushed brass tapware or light spilling through French doors.

Wherever possible, show movement: a door opening, curtains swaying or a candle being lit. Include cutaway shots of the local area, the garden in bloom or a sunset view from the terrace. Keep it short (ideally under 2 minutes) and make sure your branding is clean yet prominent. Most importantly, don't just show the house. Sell the feeling of living there. When you make buyers say, "I want that life," the home sells itself.

Key Element #3: Lifestyle Property Description that Sells the Lifestyle

The "write" words (forgive the pun) can really help the homes you list come to life on the page and stand out on Rightmove and the other property portals. We use a team of copywriters who will often interview our clients about their homes and highlight the things they love most about them, which will likely appeal to their ideal buyer, too.

When marketing a premium home, your description should go far beyond square footage and ceiling heights. It should sell the lifestyle. Think about what it feels like to live there, not just what it looks like. Is this a home where mornings begin with coffee on the sun-drenched terrace? Where long lunches are shared in a garden framed by wisteria? Or where city lights sparkle through floor-to-ceiling windows as you wind down in the evening?

Start by identifying the emotional anchors of the property – light, flow, tranquillity, grandeur, privacy – and weave those into your opening lines. Avoid clichés like "must be seen" or "deceptively spacious" and focus on crafting a narrative. Bring the reader in. Help them imagine themselves hosting dinner parties, working from the garden studio or running a bubble bath under a skylight. When you sell the dream, not just the details, you invite buyers to feel something. That's what turns curiosity into action.

A beautiful property description will tell the story of the home, tempting the buyer inside through the page and enticing them to want to see more. It's also a real client-pleaser as our sellers love to see how enthusiastically we approach describing their home and relish the opportunity to tell our copywriters how much they love it!

Expect to pay around £200 for a professionally written description of around 1000 words. At the time of writing, we are discovering more about the power of AI in our business and using tools like ChatGPT to create the ten Rightmove bullet points and to write social media posts based on a professionally written description.

Here's an easy formula you can use to help write a compelling "lifestyle" property description.

Lifestyle-Driven Property Description Formula

Use this structure to turn your property descriptions from basic to brilliant:

Step 1: Hook With Emotion or Lifestyle

Begin with a scene-setting sentence that invites the reader to join in. Focus on how it feels to live there.

Example: "Bathed in golden morning light and framed by rolling hills, this elegant country home offers a peaceful escape just moments from town life."

Step 2: Introduce the Property With Key Features

Mention the standout elements, but keep it elegant and not too list-like.

Example: "Set across 3,500 sq ft, this beautifully restored period property features five double bedrooms, expansive living spaces and a garden made for summer entertaining."

Step 3: Highlight Signature Spaces

Choose 1 to 2 areas of the home to describe in detail. Think of the kitchen, principal suite or outdoor spaces.

Example: "The heart of the home is the open-plan kitchen, complete with a marble island, Lacanche range and French doors that lead out to the wisteria-covered patio."

Step 4: Paint the Lifestyle Picture

Use language that evokes a mood and tells a story. What kind of life does this home offer?

"Whether it's hosting long lunches in the garden, curling up by the fire on crisp autumn nights or enjoying a soak with a view of the stars, every detail of this home invites relaxation and connection."

Step 5: Briefly Mention Location Highlights

Touch on transport, community, nature or convenience – just enough to anchor the dream.

"Tucked into a quiet lane just 10 minutes from the vibrant market town of Burford, this home offers the best of country living with everything you need close by."

Step 6: Finish With a Call-to-Action

Conclude with a warm and inviting prompt.

"Homes like this are rarely available – book your private viewing today and experience it for yourself."

Sample Premium Listing Description (Using the Formula)

An Idyllic Retreat on the Edge of the Cotswolds

Wake up to birdsong and sunshine streaming through sash windows, in a home where every detail feels like a quiet luxury. Nestled on the edge of a thriving Oxfordshire village, this beautifully extended four-bedroom home blends character and comfort in all the right ways.

From the welcoming flagstone hallway to the light-filled kitchen with its handcrafted cabinetry and breakfast garden views, this is a home designed for modern family living – with warmth, soul and style.

Upstairs, the principal suite offers a peaceful escape, featuring vaulted ceilings, bespoke storage and a roll-top bath overlooking open fields. Outside, a south-facing garden wraps around the home, with a wildflower lawn, fruit trees and a terrace perfect for long, lazy lunches.

Just five minutes from a bustling market town and under 90 minutes to London, this is country living without compromise.

Viewing is by appointment only – please contact Stowhill Estates to arrange a private tour.

Key Element #4: Glossy Magazine Style Brochure

Some agents will tell you that "print is dead," but we wholeheartedly disagree. In a world saturated with digital noise, a beautifully designed, magazine-style brochure offers something tangible, memorable and elevated. It signals that this home is something special.

A glossy brochure not only showcases the property's best features with care and style, but it also enhances the perceived value of the home itself. It feels considered. Premium. Aspirational. Would you rather a potential buyer walk away with a professionally designed, high-quality brochure they'll flick through again at home, or a black-and-white printout from the office copier? Or worse, just a link in an email?

In our experience, buyers tend to respond to print on an emotional level. They hold onto it. They imagine the home becoming theirs. And that emotional engagement is exactly what sells houses. A magazine-style brochure doesn't just market the property; it reflects your brand, your attention to detail and your commitment to doing things properly.

Key Element #5: Bespoke Boards & Property Logos: Branding at Its Best

For truly special homes, a standard For Sale board just doesn't do the property justice. Creating a bespoke board, one that reflects the unique character of the home, elevates the listing before a buyer even steps foot inside.

Whether it's a classic country manor, a modern architectural masterpiece or a charming thatched cottage, a tailored board signals to the world that this is no ordinary house. For an extra layer of storytelling and sophistication, consider designing a unique logo or monogram for each individual home you market. It could be inspired by the property's name, history or architectural details. Use it across the brochure, social media, video content and board to create a cohesive, high-end visual identity that buyers remember.

Not only does this set your listing apart, but it positions you as the kind of agent who goes above and beyond, someone who treats every home like a brand and every seller like a VIP.

Key Element #6: Direct Mail

When you're selling a high-value or unique home, never underestimate the power of the people already living nearby. A well-crafted, beautifully branded direct mail campaign to neighbours isn't just about attracting a buyer; it's about creating buzz in the right circles.

Often, neighbours know someone who's looking to move to the area – a friend, a family member, a colleague who's always admired the house down the road. Sending a premium postcard, folded letter or mini-brochure with a warm introduction, a few teaser images and an invitation to view or request the brochure can spark interest long before the listing hits Rightmove. And crucially, it positions you as the go-to agent for discreet, high-calibre marketing.

Done well, this kind of mail doesn't feel like junk. Instead, it feels like a personal invitation. And that small, elegant touch can open doors you didn't even know were there.

Key Element #7: Social Media Campaigns With Impact

To truly maximise a home's exposure, every agent should create a tailored social media campaign for each property. Why? Because not every buyer is actively searching on Rightmove. Some are just thinking about moving. Others are scrolling Instagram on a Sunday afternoon and stumble across the dream kitchen that nudges them to take action.

Social media allows you to capture those passive buyers – people who don't even know they're looking yet. A great campaign should include a mix of behind-the-scenes video content, reels showcasing styling or media day, carousel posts highlighting key features and even local lifestyle shots to showcase the area. It's also a brilliant opportunity to boost your personal brand.

Every home you market becomes a case study of your expertise, style and results. Done right, your social media becomes a portfolio that attracts future sellers who say, "I want that for my home." It builds your authority, increases your visibility and differentiates you from the competition, especially if they're still relying on just a couple of wide-angle shots and a standard description. So don't leave your best content trapped on a portal; share it with the world.

We've created a handy, free step-by-step social media checklist to help you ensure you get it right every time.

Visit www.eliteagentcollective.com/resources to download it, or scan the QR code located on the back of this book.

Key Element #8: Harness the Power of the Press

Rightmove is essential, but it's not the whole story. If you want to elevate your marketing and position yourself as the go-to agent for unique or high-value homes, potentially reaching a national audience, then a well-crafted press and PR campaign can be a game changer.

Why does PR matter? Well, a great media feature does three powerful things:

1. **Attracts new eyes** to the listing, especially buyers who aren't actively searching portals like Rightmove.

2. **Elevates the home's perceived status**, adding credibility and buzz.

3. **Builds your personal brand** as the kind of agent who markets homes with style, strategy and a bit of media sparkle.

What makes a property press-worthy? Not every home will be a headline, but you might be surprised at how many could be, with the right spin. Journalists want a story, not just a listing, so ask yourself:

Does the property have a fascinating history (e.g. a converted church, former bakery, or famous owner)?

Does it have unusual or luxurious features (e.g. an indoor slide, treehouse office, yoga barn, cinema room)?

Is it sustainably built or an example of eco-living done right?

Is the home part of a lifestyle shift story (e.g. a couple moving from city to country post-pandemic)?

Can it ride a seasonal trend (e.g. a thatched cottage in spring, or a ski lodge in winter)?

Your job is to frame the listing like a lifestyle feature. Bring the reader in with imagination and not just square footage. Start by targeting well-loved regional outlets, such as your local newspaper or a local glossy lifestyle magazine. For truly unique or high-end homes, target titles such as *The Sunday Times* Home section, *Country Life*, *The Telegraph Property* or *The Times Bricks and Mortar*.

If you want to pitch like a pro, remember that journalists get hundreds of emails per week. To stand out, you must make their job easy, so make sure your pitch is short, snappy and story-focused. Here's a checklist of what to include:

- A punchy subject line (e.g. "Converted railway station with secret cinema room for sale in the Cotswolds")

- A brief intro: Who you are, what the home is and why it's interesting

- A few lines highlighting the story angle (history, features, lifestyle element)

- Key property facts: price, location, unique points

- A link to the brochure or website listing

- High-resolution images (or a Dropbox/WeTransfer link)

- Your contact details and an offer to arrange interviews or viewings

Remember to be timely. Pitch seasonal homes ahead of time (e.g. cottages in spring, coastal homes in summer). Be persistent by following up gently, and be prepared to be flexible. Journalists may want a slightly different angle or request quotes from the owner.

The results of your hard work will be a property that stands out, a seller who's impressed and a buyer who never saw it coming. And importantly, an agent (you!) who's positioned as a creative, media-savvy professional with a reputation for going above and beyond.

Creating a Property Marketing Roadmap for Your Clients

One of the most effective ways to build trust with your clients – and set yourself apart from other agents – is to create a clear and visually engaging Property Marketing Roadmap. This is a step-by-step guide that outlines exactly what will happen once they instruct you: from the initial consultation and home styling day, through to professional photography, brochure production, social media promotion, PR opportunities, launch date and beyond.

It removes uncertainty, positions you as organised and strategic and gives the client a sense of control during what can be an emotional process. A great roadmap not only showcases your high standards, but it also reassures the client that their home is in expert hands and builds anticipation for each exciting milestone. Better yet, it becomes a subtle reminder of just how much work goes into a world-class campaign, and why your fee is worth every penny.

Here's a sample Property Marketing Roadmap template you can use for your own clients:

Your Property Marketing Roadmap

What to expect when you work with us, from instruction to SOLD!

1. Initial Consultation

We meet at your home to understand your goals, discuss your timeline and share our strategy for presenting and promoting your home to its fullest potential.

2. Pre-Media Styling Visit

We walk through each room with you, making recommendations on how to stage your space for maximum impact. We'll help with decluttering, repositioning furniture and identifying styling touches. You'll also receive a checklist and styling prep guide to make the process easier.

3. Media Day

Our team returns with professional photographers, videographers, drone operators (if needed) and our curated styling kit to present your home beautifully. This is a big day and the start of your home's story in the market.

4. Brochure Creation

We craft a bespoke, magazine-style brochure featuring your property's photography, floorplans and a compelling, story-driven description. We'll also include a local area lifestyle snapshot and an optional owner quote.

5. Digital & Social Campaign Launch

We create a multi-platform marketing campaign utilising high-impact social media reels, carousel posts, email marketing, and premium listing features – all strategically designed to capture attention and generate excitement.

6. PR & Press Opportunities

For homes with a unique story, we pitch to select local and national publications (e.g. *Country Life, The Sunday Times, Cotswold Life*) to reach a wider audience and elevate your home's perceived value.

7. Launch Week

Your home goes live on the portals (Rightmove, Zoopla, OnTheMarket), our client database is notified and viewings begin. You'll receive real-time updates and feedback after every appointment.

8. Offer Negotiation

Once offers come in, we negotiate fiercely on your behalf to secure the best price, terms and buyers who are serious and proceedable.

9. Sales Progression

We stay closely involved from offer to exchange, liaising with solicitors, keeping the chain moving and troubleshooting anything that might delay your sale.

10. Completion Day

The keys are handed over, the bubbly is popped and you move forward with your next chapter. And don't worry, we'll be here for anything you need, long after the sale completes.

Remember, the primary purpose of bespoke marketing is to attract sellers: new clients who you can serve, who also want the same for their homes.

Of course, bespoke property marketing also has the secondary benefit of selling homes faster and for a higher price. We know you can sell a home without these things, but bespoke marketing is a fantastic way to showcase exactly what your agency can do and attract new sellers to you.

Marketing That Moves the Needle – and Builds Your Brand

Bespoke property marketing is more than just a way to sell homes; it's a magnet for your ideal clients. It's what sets you apart from the corporate pack. It's what elevates your brand, builds your authority and justifies your fees without a flinch.

Yes, it takes more time. Yes, it costs more to do it properly. But if you want to build a business that thrives at the top end of the market, it's not just worth it – it's essential. Because when sellers see their home brought to life with thoughts, style and strategy, they'll tell their friends. They'll come back to you. And they'll expect to pay more because they've seen the difference.

This chapter has given you the blueprint. Now, it's up to you to put it into action, raise your standards and build a reputation for doing things exceptionally well. World-class marketing doesn't just sell houses. It sells you.

Chapter 10
No News Is Still News

How to Master the Art of Communication and Build Unshakeable Client Trust

Communication is the part of estate agency that most agents get horribly wrong. And yet, it's the single most powerful way to build trust, loyalty and long-term success. In the high-value homes market, where your clients are entrusting you with their biggest asset and highest hopes, *how* you communicate becomes just as important as *what* you deliver.

This chapter is about more than just returning calls or sending a weekly email. It's about showing up with presence, empathy and clarity even when there's nothing new to say. Because when your clients feel consistently seen, heard and supported, you become more than "the estate agent." You become their trusted advisor. In a world full of radio silence and robotic updates, that makes you unforgettable.

Our industry doesn't exactly have the best reputation when it comes to communication. If we had a pound for every time a seller said, "We never heard from our agent unless we chased them," we'd have a garage full of classic cars by now!

And it's not just hearsay. Research from industry watchdogs and consumer feedback confirms it: One of the biggest gripes homeowners have is poor communication. Or, more worryingly, sometimes, a total lack of it.

This is your opportunity. Want to stand out in the high-value homes market? Then you must become *that* agent who's known for impeccable, proactive and consistent communication. Not flashy, not over-the-top; just reliable, honest and high-quality. It's that simple.

Why Communication Is the Cornerstone

When you're selling someone's £1m home, you're not just shifting bricks and mortar. You're dealing with their pride and joy, their memories, their biggest asset. High-value clients expect and deserve an experience that feels bespoke, attentive and premium. And that begins with communication.

It's not about calling them once a week because your CRM told you to. It's about being a trusted advisor, a sounding board and someone who makes them feel like they're your only client, even when they're not.

Top agents don't just sell luxury homes; they sell trust. They build relationships. That all starts with the how, when and why they communicate.

Here's the golden rule we swear by:

No news is still news.

You might think, "But I've got nothing to update them on this week." Doesn't matter. Tell them that! That small act of transparency builds mountains of trust. It shows your client that you're still on the case, still thinking about them and still in control of the process.

The Industry Standard Is Shockingly Low

We've been beating this drum for years: The bar is so low in estate agency that it's practically buried underground. A client who gets a weekly update, even if it's just a voice note saying, "Hey, no viewings this week, but we've ramped up your online reach and I'll keep you posted," will think you're a superstar.

Why? Because most agents go radio silent the minute the contract is signed.

It's baffling to us. You wouldn't ignore your best friend's messages for three days straight without a response. So why ghost your client? Especially when they've trusted you with a seven-figure sale?

This industry is full of agents who mean well but execute poorly. What sets agents apart isn't just what they do; it's how they make people *feel*. And you can't make someone feel seen, heard or understood if you're not talking to them on a regular basis!

Quality Over Quantity (But Consistency Is Key)

Let's get one thing clear: Communication doesn't mean bombarding your client with meaningless updates. That's not helpful, it's annoying! What you want is quality communication, delivered consistently.

That might look like:

- A Monday morning check-in every week, whether there's news or not
- A mid-week progress update, if there's feedback from viewings
- A monthly report that outlines marketing reach, buyer interest and next steps
- A quick video message to explain a market shift in their area
- An honest, empathetic phone call if things aren't going as planned

You don't need to overthink it. Just be the agent who shows up and keeps them in the loop. Let them feel like they're part of the process, not just waiting in the wings for updates that never come.

Communication = Confidence

High-value clients want to feel confident. Confidence in the market. Confidence in their pricing. Confidence in *you*. And guess what? Communication is the bridge that delivers that confidence.

When you don't communicate, your client starts to fill in the blanks. They assume the worst. They lose trust. And once trust is gone, it's only a matter of time before they give the instruction to someone else – someone who *does* keep in touch.

You'll never lose a client because you communicated too well. But stay silent too long, and they'll start calling around. Don't give them a reason to.

Pro Tips for Next-Level Communication

Set Expectations Early

At the valuation stage, explain how and when you'll communicate. This makes you look organised and dependable from Day One.

Use Multiple Formats

Some people love a phone call. Others prefer email, WhatsApp or even Loom video updates. Ask them what works best, and tailor your approach accordingly.

Systemise It

Build your communications into your weekly rhythm. Set calendar reminders or use your CRM to trigger check-ins. Make it part of your process, not something you only do when you remember.

Be Human

Don't be robotic. Speak like a person, not a policy. "Hey John, just checking in to let you know we've had no viewing requests this week. I know it's frustrating, but I'm on it and here's what I'm doing next..." That's all they need to hear.

Why WhatsApp is Your Secret Weapon for Client Communication

If email is the business suit of communication – formal, structured, a bit stiff – then WhatsApp is your favourite cashmere jumper: relaxed, warm and easy to be around. And in a high-end estate agency, that human touch is everything.

We're in the business of relationships, not transactions. So, it makes sense to meet your clients where they actually are. For 99 % of them, that's WhatsApp.

Why WhatsApp Works

Let's break down why this simple little app can be a total game-changer for your business:

- **It's immediate.** Messages are usually read within minutes, not hours or days like email.
- **It feels personal.** WhatsApp is where people chat with family, close friends and colleagues. When you show up there, you're no longer "just the estate agent" – you're part of their inner circle.
- **You can use voice notes and video.** These formats convey tone, energy and empathy in a way no email ever could.
- **It's convenient.** You can reply on the go, keep conversations flowing and even send documents or photos if needed.

And in case you were wondering, yes, your high-value clients do use WhatsApp. Even the tech-averse ones!

The Magic of Voice and Video Notes

Email is fine for formal updates or long documents, but if you want to build trust, loyalty and connection? Use your voice.

A 30-second voice note after a viewing to say, "Just walked through with the buyer. She loved the garden but had some questions about the heating. I'll follow up and let you know."

A quick video message to explain market shift or your new pricing recommendation: "Hi Sarah, I've just seen what's gone under offer nearby. It confirms what we discussed earlier – your price is spot on. Here's what I'm doing next..."

These little messages take seconds to send, but the impact is huge. It shows care. It builds confidence. And it sets you apart from every other agent firing off templated emails once a week.

Systemise It (So You Never Drop the Ball)

Now you might be thinking, "This all sounds great, but there's no way I'll have time to do all of this consistently!" The answer: Create a simple system that automates the reminders, not the communication itself. Here's how.

Set a Weekly Comms Rhythm

Choose a set day (e.g. every Monday or Friday) to update all your clients. Block out an hour in your diary. Stick to it religiously.

Use a CRM to Prompt You

Add reminders or tasks for each client. The system reminds you; you send a short, personal message. That's the difference between "meh" and "memorable."

Create Message Templates (But Personalise the Delivery)

You can write a few flexible scripts or outlines ahead of time, just avoid sounding robotic. Even a simple line like, "Just wanted to check in – it's been a quiet week, but I've got some ideas brewing..." makes them feel like they're in good hands.

Batch Your Updates

Record all of your voice notes or videos back-to-back, then fire them out to each client. You'll save time, and they'll still feel like you've personally taken the time to reach out.

Use Broadcast Lists (Carefully)

On WhatsApp Business, you can create a broadcast list that sends the same message to multiple people individually. Ideal for a quick "here's what's happening in the market this week" update – but make sure to personalise follow-ups based on each client's situation.

When you use WhatsApp well, your communication doesn't just inform; it connects. It reassures. It builds rapport. And that's where your real value lies.

So don't overthink it, just start using it. Your clients will appreciate the effort, and your competitors will wonder why your clients never leave!

Systemise for Success

Systemising your client communication isn't just about being efficient. It's about building trust before you need it. When you show up consistently throughout the selling journey, keeping your clients informed and supported at every step, you're laying the groundwork for a relationship based on confidence and rapport. So, when things inevitably get tricky, like needing to have a difficult conversation about reducing the asking price, or when the conveyancing process turns into a bit of a horror show, you're not met with resistance or suspicion. You're met with respect.

Why? Because by then, you're not just "the estate agent." You've become their trusted advisor: the calm, capable expert who's been there every step of the way. You've communicated clearly, delivered value and never left them in the dark. So when you say, "We need to rethink our pricing strategy," they listen. When you explain that a delay in conveyancing isn't the end of the world, they believe you. Because you've earned their trust long before they've needed to lean on it. And that's what separates the average agents from the exceptional ones.

Suggested "Keep in Touch" Schedule for Sellers

Stage 1: Warm Welcome & Onboarding

Welcome Email and Gift

Timing: immediately after signing the sales agreement

Medium: email and a hand-delivered or posted gift

Focus: gratitude and excitement; reassure them they've made the right choice

Content:

- Thank them for trusting you with their home
- Let them know what to expect over the next few days
- Include a short video message (optional) from you or your team

Gift Ideas: scented candle, branded notebook, local artisan treat, handwritten note

Onboarding Email: Meet the Team and Next Steps

Timing: within 24 to 48 hours of the signed agreement

Medium: email with team photo or short welcome video

Focus: introduce the team and demystify the next steps.

Content:

- Who does what on your team (e.g. admin, negotiator, photographer)
- Timeline for professional photos, video, copywriting and market launch
- How/When they'll hear from you going forward
- Invite them to save your number on WhatsApp

Stage 2: Active Marketing Period

Weekly Updates

Timing: once per week (e.g. every Friday or Monday)

Medium: WhatsApp voice note or short email (depending on client performance)

Focus: keep them in the loop, even if there's "no news"

Content:

- Viewing the feedback summary
- Rightmove/marketing performance (views, enquiries, etc.)
- What actions you've taken this week
- What's happening in the local market
- Reassure them you're on the case

Remember that no news is still news. Never skip a week, even during quiet spells.

Monthly Marketing Review

Timing: every 4 weeks after launch

Medium: email with attached PDF report or Loom video

Focus: a more detailed check-in; explain what's working, what could improve

Content:

- Portal analytics and engagement
- Social media reach (if applicable)
- Comparison with other similar homes
- Overview of current strategy and recommendations

6-Week Strategic Review

Timing: 6 weeks after the marketing launch

Medium: face-to-face meeting (or Zoom if distance is a challenge)

Focus: big-picture review and recalibration

Content:

- What the data is telling us so far
- Strategic recommendations (this is the moment to discuss pricing if needed)
- Reassess marketing tactics (photos, wording, staging etc.)
- Reconfirm motivation and timeline
- Set clear next steps and an action plan

Pro Tip: Bring printed materials, graphs and visuals to make it feel valuable and professional, like a performance review, not a panic meeting.

Stage 3: Offer Accepted & Conveyancing

Offer Accepted Update

Timing: the day the offer is accepted

Medium: call followed by WhatsApp message and email confirmation

Focus: celebrate and set clear expectations for what comes next

Content:

- Summary of offer terms
- Introduction to sales progressor (if applicable)
- Timeline for key milestones
- List of next steps for both sides

Weekly Progress Updates During Conveyancing

Timing: every week

Medium: WhatsApp or phone call, followed by a summary email

Focus: reassurance and proactive updates on what's happening behind the scenes

Content:

- Updates from solicitors
- Chasing and problem-solving behind the scenes

- Honest conversations about expected completion dates

Stage 4: Post-Sale Follow-Up

Completion Day Celebration

Timing: Day of Completion

Medium: A phone call and delivery of a small gift or thank-you card

Focus: Celebrate the moment, reinforce your personal brand

Gift Ideas: a bottle of Champagne, a moving day survival kit, a donation to their chosen charity in their name

Post-Sale Follow Up

Timing: 2 weeks after completion

Medium: WhatsApp or email

Focus: checking in, future referrals and staying in touch

Content:

- "How's the move?"
- Offer help if they need anything local
- Ask for a testimonial or Google review
- Mention referral incentive (if applicable)

Having a communication system in place means you never leave clients wondering what's going on. It transforms what is often an emotional and stressful experience into one that feels calm, clear and well-managed. It also positions you as the go-to expert they'll rave about to their friends and come back to when they're ready to move again.

In the world of high-value estate agency, your communication is your brand. It's the inevitable thread that ties the entire experience together. You don't need to be perfect, but you do need to be present.

So repeat after us: "No news is still news."

Say it. Live it. Build a business on it.

Because when your clients feel seen and supported – even in the quiet weeks – you don't just sell houses. You become unforgettable.

The Good, The Bad and the "Go On Then"

Michael here to share a couple of stories that will hopefully illustrate the power of consistent communication (and may even make you smile!).

Communication is key in all walks of life, but it's really important (and the main reason I hear why estate agents are fired) during the marketing and sales progression of a home. I don't believe there can be too much of it, whether it's face-to-face, over the phone, via email, text or WhatsApp. No news is still news.

Regardless of the medium you use, how you communicate is paramount. Are you subservient, arrogant, meek, lacking confidence, desperate even or coming from an equal level of status? The last point is so important: You must be of equal status to your client or buyer, or you've lost, sometimes before you've even begun. This can be as simple as removing your shoes upon entering a home when not required to do so. Of course, after eight years in the estate agency game (and it's exactly that – a game) and over 30 years in sales, I have one or two stories, if not experiences, I can share with you.

A few years ago, we were approached by a potential seller of a home in a nearby village. They had seen our social media posts and loved our marketing style. We were right for them and we had attracted them, so they were right for us! This was great – the laws of attraction were working!

We had a great meeting, taking a look around their lovely, characterful home. It needed some work, which was one of the reasons we were there, to offer them advice on what to do (amazingly, we were also trusted advisors!). We were then instructed to sell their home. As soon as they'd completed the renovations, we would go to market at the agreed price of £1m.

A couple of months later, we were invited back to see what they had done, and it looked amazing – beautiful, in fact. We were looking forward to "doing our thing." Along came the media day, and the team went about their business – styling, staging, capturing photos and video. All went brilliantly. The client was thrilled with the professional images and the professionally written description. We agreed it was time to go to market, but they wanted to try a price of £1,175,000. Even though we knew this was too high, we agreed to it. First mistake. Don't forget, you're the professional here; you know what's going on in the market currently, and more importantly, you/we don't get paid until the house has received an offer and sold.

Sure enough, viewings were slow, very slow. We would update the client on a weekly basis, showing that it was underperforming compared to others on our books, and that perhaps we needed to consider the price. "No, we don't think that's the problem, let's give it more time," they said.

Time moved on, and after generating a couple of viewings, with no offers and feedback that it was a "bit rich," we held another call. "We still think the price is fine, so perhaps it's the marketing?"

"Erm, we don't feel it's the marketing as it's far superior to anyone else's."

"We think the description is too long, so please, can you reduce it?" Now, rather than standing our ground and coming from a place of confidence, not arrogance (we know how to sell homes, as this is what we do!), we agreed to reduce the wording to a bare minimum.

This is not what we do. We write the most beautiful, alluring descriptions that bring the home to life. Everyone compliments us on them to the point that the vast majority of our clients say the photos, brochure and description are so beautiful they're not sure they want to move anymore. So, why did we agree to butcher this element of our marketing!?

Immediately, we were no longer of equal standing with our client. They were now dictating to us how we should do our job. Let's not forget the biggest point here: They had initially been attracted to us *because* of our marketing, and now we were changing it at their request!

Again, the marketing edits had no impact on the interest. We held another call and advised that an Offers Over strategy of £1m (the price we'd always advised should be the marketing price) was the best way to attract a potential buyer. This was ignored. Their suggestion was that we reduce the number of images we had on show. Sometimes, this is a fair point, as some agents have far too many images, which can overwhelm people and put them off before they even arrive. Around 20 to 25 images is optimum unless it's a very large home with land, outbuildings, a swimming pool, a tennis court, etc. However, we already had only 20 images. Again, we agreed, and, against all our instincts, better judgment and experience, we reduced the images. Guess what? Nothing improved.

A few weeks later, and after another discussion about the benefit of an Offers Over £1m strategy, we were given notice. We'd lost all control and credibility with the client, and they listed with another agent, again at £1,175,000. We watched the home carefully over the coming weeks and had to smile, through gritted teeth, to see it eventually come down to £1m and then sell! Big surprise! We took some relief knowing we were right all along, but just too weak to stand by our conviction.

What we learned here is that, despite attracting them to us due to the strength of our marketing, we ourselves didn't truly believe in it, and we allowed the client to dictate how things should be done. Even after doing everything they "told us to," we still lost them and, in their minds, failed to secure a buyer for their home.

One other story for you.

In the past, if a client had written to me detailing a list of points or objections, I would always respond, answering each of their comments in line one by one! I'd look at my reply, smiling and thinking, "There, that's gotcha!"

Of course, I'd shortly get a reply knocking all of my points back into the rubble and around we'd go again. I couldn't help it, I'd have to respond, trying to make them see. But of course, people don't. Everyone has an opinion, and people want to be right.

The easiest example Lucy and I always refer back to when you can't seem to satisfy someone is TripAdvisor reviews. It could be the most luxurious, expensive hotel in the world with nearly (and here's my point) all 5-star reviews, but there will always be a handful who simply hated it, had the worst experience, etc. So, you get this everywhere, nearly all the time. It's simply not worth trying to argue or, more importantly, go down the rabbit hole they're trying to send you.

This brings me to my second example, which was with a total control freak who just loved to be the "expert negotiator" and had the last word. If I hadn't handled him (I must say, very well), with great guidance and coaching from Lucy, we would have lost them and the all-cash buyer of their £1.5m home.

The home was lovely, although it had suffered from a common compromise: It had been overdeveloped. It was too big for the plot. It had six bedrooms, six bathrooms, a huge kitchen-dining-family room, a sitting room and a study, but a very small garden. We knew it was likely to be more challenging to sell. We were also the second agent to try.

The media team did their thing, and the home went onto the market for £1.5m. Over the weeks, we had eight viewings, with most of the feedback being the same. "If only it had a larger garden." We did have an offer, though, of £1.4m, all cash, no connected sale as the buyers were relocating from Europe. The offer was rejected.

The sellers were moving to the Midlands and building a new home on a plot they had already completed. The house build had already started, so the sale of their current home was key for them to finance the rest of the build. They had received an offer of £1.35m from their previous agent, which they had rejected; however, this new offer of £1.4m was starting to suggest what the market value of the home might be.

A few days later, the buyers returned with an increased offer of £1.42 million. Great, we're getting somewhere!

This offer was rejected, with the seller stating that they had previously turned down a £1.425m offer, so they won't be accepting one lower. This was news to me, but fair enough. I was asked to go back with a counteroffer of £1.475m, which I did, along with a market-based data justification for this. They responded, sticking with their original offer of £1.42m.

Two weeks later, and after much back-and-forth negotiating, I received a Best and Final Offer of £1,437,000 (an odd number, I know, but there you go), which I presented.

The seller went into control mode. "You told me it was worth £1.5m, and your confidence in securing this amount was the reason we chose you. It's some distance from where we want or need to be, so would you be willing to reduce your fee to £15k, including VAT if we accept this offer?" Based on this offer, our fee was over £25k, including VAT, so I think you know our answer.

Firstly, unlike the majority of agents, we never value a home; we always present a pricing strategy which we discuss and agree on with our client. I could have responded in a lot of detail and moved to justification mode, however, my wife coached me not to, and we responded as follows;

Thanks for your email and the comments you raise.

It's our role and responsibility to present you with offers on your home and use the benefit of our experience to advise you on what we believe to be the best possible offer at the time. I appreciate that this can sometimes mean delivering news that is not what you had hoped.

Statistically and in our experience, the first few weeks of marketing deliver the best offers. The longer the home sits on the market, the less chance you have of achieving the asking price.

With this in mind, we suggest you give this offer due consideration. I appreciate we have another viewing lined up for tomorrow, so I suggest we catch up again after the viewing to discuss the offer on the table.

I appreciate your question about our fee and understand why you would ask; however, whichever offer you decide to accept, our fee will remain the same.

All the best,

He responded with "Noted." And then threw in, "The idea of letting it and coming back to the market in 6 to 12 months becomes appealing."

I'm sure this was to lure me into a long-drawn-out conversation and have me panicking, "Oh, he's going to come off the market!" However, after another negative viewing and some coaching (thanks, Lucy!) I went back with the tactic that he has more to lose than I do if he doesn't accept an offer that I believe will be the best one he gets: the fear of loss.

I agreed that he could absolutely rent the home for 6 to 12 months if this wouldn't restrict any capital required for his onward build, and asked him if he felt that the incoming Labour government was likely to have a positive or negative effect on the premium property market.

I ended with, "We don't speculate but offer advice based on the information on hand and on the here and now – the decision, and risk, of course, is up to you." I kept him with the feeling of being in control, and ended with, "I do need to go back to Mr & Mrs Smith regarding their offer of £1,437,500, so please let me know what you'd like to do."

He came back with another counter of £1.45m, which I presented, but they re-confirmed that their last offer was their best and final, so were sticking.

The seller came back with, "Go on then." Once agreed, he then wanted to stipulate some timelines for exchange and completion. An exchange within six weeks and completion on a specific date. This wasn't unreasonable; however, it had not been agreed upon with the buyers who were relocating from Europe, and parties would be subject to the speed of searches, surveyors, and, of course, the solicitors. We all agreed to use our best endeavours to meet this timeframe.

Everything was progressing well, the survey was okay, some items were agreed to be purchased and the solicitors were doing their thing. We just needed the funds to be gathered from multiple sources and from overseas, so rigorous anti-money laundering checks.

The unilateral "deadline" for exchange came and went. The solicitors were still finalising a few details and the funds were being transferred. However, as they were spread across multiple accounts and stocks, it was taking a little longer than hoped. Nevertheless, the buyers were on top of it – I was confident in that. This did not stop my client or his solicitor from applying so much pressure onto the buyer's solicitor that people started to get pissed off.

We were a day late, and my client suggested that we re-list the home on the open market. I suggested that this might provoke the wrong response from the buyer, as we were so close to exchange. Of course, the decision was his.

He agreed, but then suggested the completion date would be moved to a date they couldn't meet. Another challenge. *Great!*, I thought. This went on, back and forth via the solicitors, as the buyers had asked that we not contact them anymore, as they were getting so frustrated with the process. I knew they were doing all they could. They were waiting for one transfer from a German bank, which required an AML check, and this was taking longer than anyone had anticipated, but was outside of our control. My client hated not being in control.

The buyers proposed a completion date just five days after the initial one. My client couldn't do that, for no other reason that I could see other than just being difficult. They were moving into a rental which was vacant and already secured. However, they were now insisting that the exchange of contracts take place before all the funds had been verified. The buyer refused to do this just in case there was a timing issue, and completion came before all the funds had cleared into the UK. Don't forget, with Stamp Duty, this was over £1.5m

I suggested we move to an exchange with a movable completion date. Of course, my buyer needed to think about this.

Next, I was advised that we were ready to exchange and guess what, with this excellent news and awaiting authority to exchange from my client, he responded via email with, "Not sure. We are discussing our options." Unbelievable!

Eventually, we heard that the exchange had taken place. This news came from the buyer's solicitor, not our client or their solicitor, and the completion date agreed upon was the one originally requested.

I never heard from them again, apart from a request from his wife for some copies of our beautiful brochures.

Sometimes, people must feel in total control, but in doing so, they can end up standing in their own way. He nearly lost his sale and the highest offer to date. Fortunately, thanks to the patience of the buyers and how we managed him, the deal went through. It wasn't easy, though, but a lot was learned!

Communication Is Your Currency

This is a final reminder that words are your most powerful tool and investment.

In a world where the industry standard for communication is disappointingly low, your ability to connect, genuinely and consistently, is your secret weapon. Communication isn't a box to tick. It's the thread that weaves trust through every stage of the journey, from instruction to completion. It's what earns you the right to have tough conversations and keeps clients loyal, even when things get rocky. Whether it's a quick WhatsApp voice note, a face-to-face review or a heartfelt phone call during a quiet week, your presence matters more than perfection.

Systemise your touchpoints, personalise your approach and never forget: No news is still news. Get this right, and you'll sell more than houses – you'll sell peace of mind. And that, in our world, is priceless.

Chapter 11
Ninja Negotiation

How to Master the Art of Negotiation and
Maximise Every Sale

This chapter is about mastering the real art of negotiation: the mindset, the tools and the real-world strategies that allow you to command higher prices, protect your clients' interests, and justify every inch of your fee. Elite estate agents don't just market homes; they masterfully negotiate them. Your ability to negotiate is arguably the single most important skill that separates the good from the elite.

We know from experience that lots of agents feel a bit "icky" about negotiating, but it is literally your job! We promise you that committing to mastering this skill will pay dividends, both in terms of your bank balance and self-confidence. So, if you take one thing from this chapter, let it be this: Your ability to negotiate isn't just a skill; it's your superpower. And it's the ultimate weapon that will separate you from the rest of the pack. It's what makes you world-class versus ordinary.

Great negotiation is how you protect your clients. It's how you command your fees. It's how you create win-win outcomes that don't just feel good, but actually *are* good for everyone involved. We discuss the power of great marketing to sell a home throughout this book, but the truth is, you can have stunning marketing, gorgeous lifestyle photography and the slickest social media feed on the block. But if you freeze as soon as an offer lands, or you default to email ping-pong between buyer and seller, then you're not truly negotiating, you're just relaying messages. And guess what? Message takers don't command premium fees.

If this chapter makes you feel uncomfortable, good. Get out of your comfort zone and read on. Then, after that, let us offer you some reassurance: Great negotiation isn't about being aggressive, clever or trying to "get one over" on the other person. Negotiations are about emotional control, tactical empathy and calm authority. As our mentor Matt Elwell says, "The best closers don't push. They guide. They ask. They understand. And then they lead people to great decisions."

How would it feel for you as an agent to have some brilliant ninja negotiating tools in your pocket? Tools that make you feel aligned and help you consistently achieve the best possible outcome for your client, whilst leaving the buyer feeling like they've won too? That's what we want to give you in this chapter.

Whether you're handling multiple offers, calming nervous clients or dealing with last-minute demands, your skill as a negotiator is what makes or breaks the deal – and builds your reputation as a high-value agent who's worth every penny.

Why Negotiation Is the Ultimate Differentiator

Any agent can list a house. They can stick it on Rightmove, take a few half-decent photos, print off a floor plan and call it a day. They might even run a social post or two with a filter slapped on for good measure.

But not every agent can *negotiate* a premium sale.

And that's the difference between someone who merely facilitates the process and someone who actually creates value.

Here's the truth: Your negotiation skills are what ultimately justify your fee. They're what transform you from a "nice-to-have" into a "must-have." They're what position you as the protector of your client's equity, the guardian of their bottom line and the reason they walk away smiling and telling all their neighbours to call you.

Negotiation is where your fee is earned – not just in theory, but in cold, hard numbers.

Let's say you charge a 1.5% fee. Now your prospective client might say, "That's expensive - the other agent has quoted me 1%." But let's say you achieve 101% of the asking price. The other agent charges 1% but secures only 94% of the asking price.

On a £2 million home, here's how that plays out:

- Your result: £2.02m sale price – £30,300 fee = £1,989,700 to the client
- Their result: £1.88m sale price – £18,800 fee = £1,861,200 to the client

That's a difference of over £128,000 in your client's pocket.

And guess what? They don't care that your brochure had gold foil. They care that you just made them six figures richer. That's negotiation mastery.

Because what you're doing isn't just *accepting* an offer. You're *crafting* one. You're managing the psychology of all parties. You're knowing when to hold firm and when to create movement. You're navigating egos, emotions and spreadsheets – often at the same time, and in the same phone call.

You're not just representing your client. You're *advocating* for them and in a way that measurably improves their outcome.

That's what makes you indispensable.

That's what makes you worth more, not less.

And that's what gives you the confidence to say, "Yes, my fee is 1.5%. And yes, I'm worth every penny, because here's the value I bring to the table."

When you master negotiation, you no longer have to justify your fee. Your results speak for you.

The Mindset of a Ninja Negotiator

If you've come with us on the journey so far in this book, you'll know by now that we always start with mindset, so it will come as no surprise that we put mindset front and centre here too. So, before we discuss tactics, let's cover mindset, because this is where elite negotiation begins.

And we're not talking about cheesy positive affirmations or awkward power poses (although Lucy's a big fan of adopting the "Superwoman" pose for a few minutes before a particularly challenging negotiation. Ask her about it!). What we're talking about is that internal edge that sets the 1% elite agent apart.

Why Mindset Matters

Let's face it, negotiation is an emotional business. There's money on the table, futures are being shaped, pressure is coming from all angles, these are make-or-break decisions and there in the middle of it all is you. Everyone is looking to you to be the superhero who can make the deal happen for them. And if your mindset is shaky, everything (and everyone) else wobbles with it.

Your mindset is the lens through which you interpret every word, pause and reaction. It's not just how you think, it's how you perceive. The same offer, tone of voice or moment of silence can feel entirely different depending on your internal state. If your mindset is grounded, you'll see a long pause as a strategic move. If your mindset is anxious, you'll see it as rejection. If you're confident, a low offer feels like an opening gambit. If you're insecure, it feels like an insult.

This is why mindset isn't a soft skill; it's the filter that shapes everything else.

Imagine wearing scratched sunglasses all day. Everything looks a little distorted, a little darker, a little off. Now imagine showing up to a negotiation with a lens clouded by fear, pressure or doubt. You'll misread tone. You'll assume the worst. You'll react instead of respond. And that's when deals go sideways.

But if you walk in with a clear lens – one polished with preparation, belief in your value and emotional regulation – you can read the room with precision. You'll spot the real objection hiding behind the question. You'll hear the opportunity in the silence. You'll stay three steps ahead because you're not clouded by your own internal chatter.

In negotiation, perception *is* power. And mindset is what sharpens that perception.

So, before you worry about tactics, focus on your lens. Is it clear? Is it calm? Is it helping you see the truth in the room, or distorting it?

What Kind of Mindset Should You Adopt?

Just to be clear, the mindset work is an ongoing practice. It's not something you can just wake up one day and decide to adopt. It takes commitment, practice and time, and it involves constantly checking in with yourself and asking great questions. A good place to start cultivating a great mindset is by adopting these three key traits that we believe lead to a Ninja Negotiator mindset.

Calm Certainty

No matter what curveballs are thrown your way, be they cheeky low offers, emotional meltdowns just at the point of exchange, last-minute demands to throw in the hot-tub (been there, done that, lost the deal), your calm becomes the anchor in the storm. Remember that Rudyard Kipling poem? "If you can keep your head when all about you are losing theirs and blaming you..."? That's the kind of energy you need to embody. No matter what frantic energy is going on around you, if you can keep your composure and calm certainty, you'll inspire trust and confidence between all parties.

It's true that in any negotiation, the most emotionally regulated person holds the power. It's why some people are so great at playing poker. When emotions are high, your steady presence brings clarity and control. You don't react. Instead, you respond.

Collaborative Curiosity

Remember: This is about creating a win-win for all parties and not winning at the expense of the other party. It's about keeping everyone focused on the big picture, uncovering what everyone really wants (usually it's actually the same thing!) and working creatively towards a solution. Instead of dismissing the demanding buyer as an arsehole, try approaching the situation with curiosity: What's really driving this buyer? What's the seller most afraid of? What's the hidden leverage I can work with?

The best negotiators are detectives, not debaters. They ask more than they tell. They listen. Then they uncover what matters most to the other party and work from there.

Quiet Authority

You don't need to shout about your value when you know your value. This kind of strong mindset stems from preparation, experience and a firm belief in the value you bring to the table. You're not there to please everyone. You're there to protect your client's interests and guide both parties to a win-win outcome.

When you believe in your ability to deliver outstanding outcomes, you're immune to lowball offers or pushback on your fee. You exude calm, quiet authority.

Tactical Empathy (A.K.A. Your Secret Superpower)

Chris Voss, a former FBI hostage negotiator, popularised the term "tactical empathy." Before you roll your eyes and say, "Yes, but I'm selling a four-bed in Henley, not rescuing hostages from a Somali warlord," bear with us.

We know handling property offers is slightly different to life-or-death hostage negotiations... but the principle remains the same.

Tactical empathy is the ability to truly understand another person's perspective without compromising your own. It's about stepping into their emotional world, even just for a moment, so they feel seen, heard and understood. And that changes everything.

Because here's the deal: People don't move forward when they feel unheard. They dig in. They resist. They go silent. But when someone feels understood, they soften. The temperature drops. Defensiveness turns into dialogue. And that's where the magic happens.

Tactical empathy doesn't mean you agree. It doesn't mean you cave. It means you recognise the emotion behind the behaviour, and then use that insight to guide the conversation forward with calm authority.

So, how do you *do* it? By using the following tools.

Mirroring

This one's simple but oddly effective. You repeat the last few words they've said in a questioning tone to draw out more information and show you're really listening.

Buyer: *"It's just not worth that much."*

You: *"Not worth that much?"*

Watch what happens next. They'll almost always explain, justify or soften their position. You're not arguing. You're encouraging them to open up.

Labelling

This is where you name the emotion or motivation you're picking up on.

"It sounds like you're worried about overpaying."

"It seems like you're feeling rushed into making a decision."

"It looks like you're unsure whether this is the right time to commit."

Labels defuse tension. They show empathy. And funnily enough, once someone hears their feelings reflected back to them, they often feel less attached to them.

Validation

Here, you acknowledge their perspective as reasonable, even if you don't agree with it. It looks like:

"I can see why you'd feel that way."

"That makes total sense, especially given the market conditions."

"Anyone in your shoes might feel exactly the same."

Validation is powerful because it builds trust, and trust is the currency of every successful negotiation.

When you combine these techniques, you create an environment where people feel safe enough to be honest. And honesty is what allows you to guide the conversation with integrity and influence.

Elite agents don't win because they overpower the other side. They win because they *understand* the other side better than anyone else in the room, and then use that understanding to craft a win-win outcome.

That's tactical empathy in action.

And no, you're not rescuing hostages. But let's be honest. When a buyer is threatening to pull out over a fridge-freezer or a seller is having a full-blown breakdown over a completion date, it can sometimes feel just as intense!

So channel your inner negotiator. Get curious, not combative. Lead with empathy, and you'll always stay in control.

A Real-World Negotiation: When Multiple Offers Go Wrong

Let us take you into a particularly challenging negotiation we handled post-COVID.

We were instructed on a beautiful cottage in the Cotswolds after two other agents had failed to do so. The sellers were lovely, but disheartened with the process of trying to sell their home, which they had lovingly (and expensively) extended over the years. Why didn't it sell with the previous two agents? We put it down to the snob factor, as the home was opposite some local authority homes that didn't match the "ideal" Cotswolds vibe that discerning London buyers were looking for.

We relaunched the property using our trademark superior bespoke marketing, which includes beautiful lifestyle photography and a video espousing the wonderful location and community. The relaunch price was at £1.1m, knowing they'd accept £1.05m and not a penny less.

Soon enough, we received a strong offer at £1.075m. The buyers were kind, hopeful and motivated, even if their purchase was contingent on the sale of their business. Our clients agreed to go with them.

Then, a buying agent called. She had cash clients from the US. They really want to see the property and move as quickly as possible if they like it. This was a common scenario during and after the COVID-19 pandemic, as many people sought to leave city life behind and escape to the countryside. Generally, we love working with buying agents, as they typically work with serious, well-qualified buyers who have paid them for their search services, making them a good bet.

They viewed quickly and fell in love with the home. An offer of £1.125m (£50k over the first offer!) arrived in our inbox minutes later.

Now came the tricky part.

Despite the US buyers' speed and their all-cash status, something felt off. They were *pushy*. But £50k more than the asking price was hard to ignore, and ultimately, our clients chose them. We delivered the hard news to the original buyers, who were understandably gutted.

We went back to the original couple and let them know that, unfortunately, another offer had come in that was higher than theirs. They were naturally upset that another viewing had taken place, which we understood; however, we were still in the due diligence stage, so the home was available at that time. They explained that their offer of £1,075,000 was as high as they were prepared to go. But they really wanted the home and, if needed, would obtain a bridging loan while the company sale was being processed.

After a lengthy conversation with our clients, during which we discussed the position of both parties and our gut feelings about the second couple, they couldn't get past the additional £50k the new offer would provide, and we couldn't blame them. So, after the proof of funds check, we went back via the buying agent with the news that her client's offer had been accepted and then had to give the bad news to the original couple, who were very upset. "Don't kill the messenger," I thought.

We don't make the decisions, but of course, we have to deliver the news. People often feel that we're to blame if or when another offer comes in, although we're legally obliged to forward any offers right up to the point of exchange of contracts. It doesn't stop you feeling bad for them, though.

A few days went by, and the US buyers were demanding deadlines for exchange and completion, which our clients were jumping through hoops to confirm they could meet, and a list of fixtures and fittings was agreed, as part of the purchase price. We were all regularly reminded how much over the asking price they were paying. Solicitors were instructed, and then things went quiet – too quiet.

A few days passed, and we received a call from the buying agent to say that their client had decided it wasn't for them after all and had withdrawn their offer. *Utter bastards*, we thought! Push in to see a home where an offer had already been accepted, decide they wanted it, offer over the asking price, and once in control, pull out. We wish the English property buying process were like the US or even Scotland, where, once an offer has been accepted, you've basically exchanged.

We made the call to the original couple, hoping they hadn't found anything else and praying they would actually speak with us, which they did. We had to endure some emotional rants, but at the end of the call, they confirmed that their offer still stood, provided our clients stopped all viewings and accepted their offer in full. They agreed, so we could proceed. Hallelujah!

Off we went again. This time, everything progressed through to exchange, although things did get a tad stressful for all involved at this point.

Parties were looking at a same-day exchange and completion, but the buyers, against the advice of their solicitor, agreed to exchange on their sale before they had exchanged on our home, their onward, so they had broken the chain with potentially nowhere to go.

What added to this was that on the day we were due to exchange and complete on our client's home, the buyers completed on their sale and had moved out! They were now en route to what would be their new home before we had even exchanged. Risky and not something anyone would ever recommend!

After numerous frantic phone calls with the solicitors, all of whom agreed that this was the buyers' fault and not their problem, the exchange took place, but not the completion. There was a delay in transferring the completion funds. At this point, the buyers were now sitting in the driveway, along with the removal men, shouting down the phone at us, saying we needed to complete it now!

We chased the solicitors – that's all we could do – and we did this all afternoon. Our clients had moved out, as though everything would be ready, but until completion had taken place, we could not hand over the keys. The buyers were frantically calling us, saying, "The house is ours, if you don't bring us the keys now, we will break down the door!" We politely and strongly advised them that this would be illegal and that the solicitors were working on it, and that they needed to wait. They waited, not patiently, and the phone calls and threats of breaking in continued – then it was time for the solicitors to go home.

The buyers literally had nowhere to go – they had completed on their sale and were sat on the drive of their soon-to-be new home. The removal men left, so a storage fee was also due, adding to their woes. The buyer was still threatening to break in, with his wife and us trying to placate him, whilst also advising that if he did, we'd have no choice but to call the police.

Fortunately, and unbelievably, there was an Airbnb next door that was available, so the buyers spent the night there, probably questioning their own actions. We doubt they slept much, if at all. The next day, the solicitors, after a good night's sleep, returned to their desks and completion took place, so the key was delivered to much relief of us, the buyers (who had calmed down a bit but did look a mixture of tired and hungover) and the fed-up-looking removal men.

This element is not particularly relevant to the overall point we're trying to make, but it demonstrates that, sometimes, when things are challenging, lots can add to it. You just have to keep calm and focus on your job, as well as be a counsellor, police officer, marriage counsellor and the best negotiator in the world.

The real point of this story is the handling of multiple offers. Whilst none of us have a crystal ball, your clients will most likely ask you which one they should choose. Now, gut feel is very powerful, but it doesn't always hold up against cash, especially when it comes to more cash and then no chain. What we have seen over the years is that men, typically, like to win, so they will do all they can to secure the purchase, whether that's with a higher offer or better timelines. Once they have, and are in control, they either have buyer's remorse and so re-negotiate after the survey, where anything can be leveraged negatively, or are a complete pain in the arse throughout the whole process. Or worse (if that is possible), they pull out altogether, leaving you with nothing and having to start all over again, potentially finding a better buyer but restarting the clock to getting paid.

We now try to secure the first acceptable offer if there are a few days between receipt of offers, as the "late to the table" people tend to be more accepting of this and are great backups should anything go wrong. If multiple offers have been received over a shorter timeframe, where due diligence has not been completed, we give all parties 24 to 48 hours to submit their best and final offers, providing everyone with an equal opportunity. Once these are in hand, we can sit with the sellers and make an informed (as best as possible) decision. This has worked well for us, and people tend to respect a formal but open process.

Always be wary of overly eager or pushy buyers – 80% of the time they will bite you in the arse!

Key Learnings and How You Can Apply Them

Here's what we've taken from that experience, and how you can apply it in your own agency.

Don't let emotion cloud strategy. Pushy buyers may offer more, but they often come with complications. Trust your instincts when something feels off and strike a balance between financial upside and risk.

Be the voice of calm. When things get tense, your ability to stay composed is your superpower. Calm, confident agents are trusted agents.

Use formal structures with multiple offers. We now use a 24- to 48-hour "best and final" process when multiple offers arrive in a short timeframe. It levels the playing field and gives clarity to your clients.

Guard the first offer carefully. We've learned that the first acceptable offer, especially if made in good faith, often ends up being the one that sticks. Late, over-the-odds offers are riskier than they appear.

Over-communicate and educate. Most clients don't understand what really goes into negotiation. Educate them. Discuss the pros and cons of each offer with them, not just the numbers.

Tactical Tools to Use in Your Negotiations

Negotiation can feel like a high-stakes game of poker where everyone's bluffing, no one wants to fold, and someone's always hiding a wildcard.

But with the right tactics, you can lead the game without breaking a sweat. Below are three of our most battle-tested techniques, which are simple, effective and easy to implement today. No special gadgets or MI5 training required.

The Flinch (A Classic That Still Works Wonders)

The flinch is the oldest trick in the book. It still works because it taps into basic human psychology. When someone throws out a cheeky offer ("We'll start at £850k"), your immediate reaction tells them everything they need to know about whether they're in the right zone or the wrong postcode entirely.

You don't rage, you don't scoff and you definitely don't start explaining why the offer is ridiculous. You just pause. Eyebrows up. Slight tilt of the head. A small, audible "hmm."

That's it.

It says, "Oof, not even close," without you having to utter a single confrontational word. And more often than not, the other party fills the silence with something like, "Well, we're flexible..." or "We'd be willing to go up if..."

Why? Because your non-verbal response created just enough discomfort to make them second-guess themselves, but not so much that they dig in their heels.

Think of it as polite shock. Less, "Are you kidding me?" and more, "Oh... interesting." You're signalling that the ball isn't even in the right stadium, but you're still at the table.

Calibrated Questions (Your Jedi Mind Trick)

Calibrated questions are one of the slickest tools in the Ninja Negotiator's kit, and Chris Voss would absolutely approve. These are open-ended, how-and-what style questions that gently nudge the other party into solving their own objection.

Instead of you saying, *"That won't work,"* you ask:

"How would you like me to present that to the seller?"

"What flexibility is there if the seller is able to meet your ideal timeline?"

"What's the main thing stopping you from moving forward today?"

These questions do three things:

1. **Shift control.** Now *they* have to do the thinking.

2. **Diffuse tension.** You're not saying no; you're exploring options.

3. **Reveal real priorities.** Because the first objection is rarely the real one.

The key is tone. You're not interrogating. You're gently inviting them to explore solutions. Ideally, ones that work for everyone.

And bonus points: If someone says, *"I need to speak to my partner,"* try asking:

"What do you think they'll need to see or hear in order to feel confident moving forward?"

That one's saved more than a few deals from the graveyard of indecision.

Scenario Planning (Because Nobody Makes Great Decisions When Panicked)

This is where you earn your fee as a calm, trusted advisor, not just someone who books viewings and forwards Rightmove links.

Scenario planning involves helping your clients consider the ripple effects of each decision, from the best-case scenario to the worst-case scenario and everything in between.

Let's say a seller wants to hold out for another £50k. Rather than just agreeing (or panicking), you guide them:

"Let's walk through what happens if we reject this offer and don't get another one this month. What would that mean for your onward plans?"

"If we go back to the buyer with a counter, what's the risk they walk? And how would you feel about that?"

"What would it look like to complete in 6 weeks instead of 12? Would that ease the pressure or create more?"

You're not fearmongering. You're not pushing. You're simply illuminating the path ahead. You're helping your client stay out of emotional reactivity and make calm, confident decisions.

Think of yourself as a strategy sat-nav. You don't tell them where to go, rather, you show them all the possible routes, with traffic warnings included.

These tools – The Flinch, Calibrated Questions and Scenario Planning – are your tactical advantage. They work because they make people feel heard, give them space to think and help everyone stay emotionally regulated. And when you're the one facilitating that kind of clarity, you're no longer just an estate agent.

You're a dealmaker.

You Don't Need to Be a Jedi – Just Start Practising

If your palms got a bit sweaty reading this chapter, good. That means it matters.

Negotiation is where deals are won, fees are earned and reputations are built. It's also the part of the job that most agents quietly dread, because they've never been taught how to do it well. They think they need to be slick, aggressive, ultra-persuasive or born with some magical gift of the gab.

Spoiler alert: You don't.

You don't need to be a Jedi. You don't need to be the loudest voice in the room. You don't need decades of experience. What you need is the right mindset, the right tools and the willingness to practise imperfectly, and often.

Because that's how real Ninja Negotiators are made. Not in boardrooms, but in living rooms. In car parks. On awkward phone calls. In stressful WhatsApp groups. With buyers who ghost, sellers who wobble and survey results that land like grenades.

What separates the elite agents from the average isn't charm or cleverness. It's emotional control. Curiosity. Clarity. The ability to hold your nerve when everyone else is losing theirs and blaming you for it.

So, let's recap what we've covered:

Your mindset is everything. It's the lens through which you interpret the deal. The sharper the lens, the better your decisions.

Tactical empathy is your secret superpower, allowing you to understand the other side without compromising your own position.

Tools like The Flinch, Calibrated Questions and Scenario Planning are simple, practical and wildly effective.

Real-life negotiation is messy, but with the right structure and a steady hand, you can lead like a pro.

You're not here to pass messages. You're here to elegantly move the deal forward.

And if all else fails, remember this:

You've already got what it takes. You care about your clients. You're committed to getting them the best result. You're not here to play small; you're here to lead with heart and skill.

So practise. Mess it up a few times. Learn what works for you. Keep calm. Keep learning. And keep sharpening your edge.

Because you, my friend, are not just an estate agent.

You're a Ninja Negotiator.

And your clients are lucky to have you in their corner.

Chapter 12
Always Be Marketing

The Habit That Builds (or Breaks) Your Business

There's one habit that separates thriving estate agents from those constantly scrambling for their next instruction. It's not charm, talent or even negotiation skill (though those help). It's this: consistent, relentless marketing, even when your calendar is packed.

If you're serious about selling high-value homes, marketing isn't optional. It's your daily, non-negotiable priority. The habit is to consistently show up in the market, even when you're already busy with instructions.

In this chapter, we'll show you why consistent marketing is the lifeline of your business, share the hard lessons we learned from getting it wrong and give you a practical roadmap to keep your pipeline full, without relying on panic or adrenaline.

The Feast and Famine Trap

Most agents operate like this:

They start with a huge marketing push – letters, social posts, door knocking and networking. It works! Appointments roll in, listings get secured, homes go live, offers come through and sales complete.

Then… the wheels fall off.

They've been so busy servicing existing clients, they've stopped looking for new ones. The diary dries up. Income stalls. Cue another frantic round of marketing – and the rollercoaster begins again.

Sound familiar?

We know the ride well. We call it "Feast and Famine," and let us tell you, it's thrilling for all the wrong reasons.

Our Wake-Up Call: When the Pipeline Vanished

In 2021, we were flying. As soon as lockdown restrictions were lifted, our phone started ringing off the hook with sellers wanting to move and buyers desperate to escape the city and enjoy a taste of rural life in Oxfordshire.

We literally could not keep up with the demand, and our days were filled with a flurry of viewings, more offers than we could have ever wished for, and sales at well over the asking price. Buyers even queued out of the door on one of our homes! Homes went under offer in a matter of days, and we could not get them on the market fast enough. In fact, some were sold without ever being listed on Rightmove.

This was how we'd always imagined estate agency would be! Easy, fun and effortless, with the money just flowing into our account. In 2021, we had our best ever year with revenues of nearly £500,000 without doing any marketing for six straight months. It felt like bliss at the time. We had finally made it!

We were soon brought back to earth with a bump. In the whirlwind of delivering client service, our marketing efforts dried up. Honestly, we didn't think we needed to do it, figuring the momentum would just carry us. We felt like we had "made it" and assumed the phone would just keep ringing.

It didn't.

By January 2022, we had literally run out of properties to sell. Yes, we'd had a massive payday bonanza, but we now had just two homes on the market, no instructions and no valuations in the diary.

We'd turned off the engine, and now we were coasting to a stop.

It was a huge wake-up call. We had stopped lead generation completely for so long that our list of prospects had dried up. We won't go too deep into the details of 2022, other than to say that we spent most of the year on the bottom loop of the rollercoaster, and went from making a huge profit in 2021 to a painful £250,000 loss in 2022.

But as with all things in business and life, our greatest failures have also been our greatest learning experiences, and we are grateful for them.

It was a brutal, humbling experience. But it taught us something priceless: Never stop marketing. Ever.

We now know that no matter how busy we are, we will never, ever stop marketing. And what's more, we've now developed a lead generation system that operates 24/7, 365 days a year, generating a steady stream of valuations into our diary without our need to be present.

When Desperation Leads to the Wrong Clients

That same year, the dry spell led us to take on a listing we should've walked away from. The market had shifted. As we sold homes, we weren't being invited to new listing appointments. Other agents were fighting tooth and nail for instructions, and so were we. It was a scrappy and uncertain time, and we were all eager to win whatever we could, as no one knew when the market might improve.

We were invited to a listing appointment at a semi-detached cottage in one of our local villages. Nice enough, but not our usual. Our sweet spot is unique and beautiful homes between

£700k and £3m – properties that truly benefit from our high-impact marketing. But given how little stock we had, we decided to go for it.

The sellers had previously turned down an offer of £640,000 and regretted it. We suggested that their home might achieve up to £670,000 and proposed an "Offers Over" strategy to attract maximum interest and create some competition. Our proposal was to launch at "Offers Over £650,000." They agreed, and we got to work.

Then came the red flags.

A few days later, the wife rang us to say that they didn't feel we were "the right fit" and that she didn't understand our marketing approach. Instead, they would be instructing a local agent to market their home.

Unfortunately, at this point, our competitive instincts kicked in. We were low on stock, had bills to pay and our egos were bruised. Instead of really considering whether this was a good client for us, we went into full-on "must win" mode. After a long conversation, we persuaded them to stay. We launched with gorgeous imagery, nailed the strategy and lined up 15 viewings on the first weekend.

Pretty soon, we had multiple offers on the table and we were buzzing. But instead of celebrating, our clients were furious. They accused us of underpricing the home. Said we'd "damaged" it online. Gave notice.

We were floored.

We'd negotiated multiple offers. We had followed the plan they had agreed to. The strategy had delivered results. The house looked incredible and we had secured a proceedable offer of £680,000 – £40k over their previous best. But they were still unhappy.

Still, we soldiered on. We negotiated with every interested party whilst dealing with constant resistance from the sellers, unsolicited advice from other agents and input from their son in Dubai, who, unsurprisingly, agreed with Mum and Dad.

When we congratulated them on completing their sale, their response was, "A rather strange sentiment considering the circumstances!" Ouch!

To top it off, their solicitor claimed there was a "dispute" and they wouldn't pay our fee. It took five angry emails and five separate instalments to get paid.

Lesson learned.

If we're truly honest, we'd always known that they weren't the right clients for us. They'd only agreed reluctantly to our approach and only after we'd persuaded them hard. We took them on because we were desperate. Because we'd stopped marketing. And because we said "yes" when we should've said "no." In a stronger market, we likely would not have taken them on. However, that short-term decision led to months of self-doubt, stress, and soul-searching.

Desperation Is the Enemy of Good Decisions

When you're not consistently marketing and generating a steady stream of potential clients, you're setting yourself up for moments of anguish just like this. It's in those quiet spells that you're most vulnerable to saying "yes" to the wrong clients.

When your pipeline is empty, you say yes to clients who micromanage, haggle and drain your energy. And the worst part? They can smell the desperation. It shows up in your tone, your negotiations and your willingness to bend. The more anxious you are about having too few instructions, the more you'll encounter potential clients who ask you to discount your fee or try to get you to agree to things you're not comfortable with.

This sort of reactive mindset leads to sleepless nights around cash flow, missed opportunities to grow and a poorer experience for your clients when you are stretched too thin.

Darren Hardy calls it "The Entrepreneurial Rollercoaster." Hustle, win, crash, panic, repeat. And it's not sustainable.

We love rollercoasters. But not in our business.

Today, we've built a marketing engine that hums along quietly in the background. It generates valuations every week, attracts our dream clients and keeps our pipeline healthy, rain or shine.

Build the Machine That Feeds You

So, how do you get off the rollercoaster and onto the smooth, steady track of predictable growth?

You build a system. An engine that runs smoothly, allowing you to stay in control and attract your ideal clients. This will allow you to stop chasing and start choosing.

Michael Port, in his book *Book Yourself Solid*, highlights that many service professionals fall into this trap because they lack a reliable client attraction system. He recommends keeping at least three lead-generation strategies running at all times. "You can't wait until you're hungry to start hunting," he says. "You have to always be building the system that feeds you."

Building this machine starts with a classic framework, which you can use as the foundation of your marketing system. Let's break it down.

The 3 M's of Marketing

Market: Who Are You Speaking To?

To attract a steady stream of leads, you must be laser-focused on who you want to work with. Remember that not every seller is your ideal client, so it's essential to define your niche clearly. Ours is:

- Professionals, entrepreneurs and downsizers selling £1m+ homes

- Sellers who value high-level marketing and will pay for it
- Those disillusioned with traditional agents

Message: What Are You Saying?

Once you know your ideal client, your message must speak directly to their pain points, desires and decision-making drivers. Think about what sort of conversations they're having over the dinner table. What keeps them up at night? Speak to their pain points and aspirations.

Great messaging positions you as a trusted advisor, focuses on the desired outcomes of your sellers, uses authority, testimonials and case studies and differentiates you brilliantly from the competition.

Remember to lead with empathy. It's not about shouting the loudest about how great you are; it's about knowing your audience so well that they feel like the message was written just for them.

Medium: Where Are You Showing Up?

The medium is the channel through which you deliver your message to the market. For consistency, you need multiple touchpoints working simultaneously. You could choose from:

- Email marketing, to nurture past clients and future sellers
- Social media, for building brand awareness and sharing behind-the-scenes stories

- Direct mail, for high-converting letters to specific postcodes or homeowners

- Video content, for building trust and authority faster

- Local networking/events, for building a profile in your community

Pick two to three core mediums to focus on and systemise them so you can ensure your messages are getting out there consistently. Dan Kennedy, in his book *No B.S. Direct Marketing*, emphasises the importance of utilising measurable, repeatable marketing channels. "The worst number in business is one," he says, "one stream of traffic, one marketing tactic, one source of leads – you must diversify and systemise."

Build a Marketing System That Works Without You

A system is anything that works without requiring daily attention. Here's how to get off the rollercoaster and onto the runway of predictable growth:

Batch and Schedule Your Marketing

Set aside one or two days per month to plan and create your marketing assets. Schedule everything in advance, including social posts, email newsletters, blogs and even handwritten letters, if possible. You can choose a theme for each month and build all your content around it (e.g. "7 Reasons to Sell in September" or "Get Set to Sell in Spring").

Automate Where Possible

There's a huge choice of email software out there that can help you automate your marketing and create email nurture sequences to ensure you're communicating with your clients and prospects in a consistent way. You can also use the power of AI to help you create automated follow-ups, call-backs or send out market updates to prospects.

Outsource or Delegate

As Hardy says, "The greatest entrepreneurs don't do more, they do less better." Hire a VA, copywriter or local marketer to help you execute your marketing consistently.

Chet Holmes echoes this in *The Ultimate Sales Machine*, where he talks about the importance of "pig-headed discipline." He recommends relentlessly marketing to your ideal clients with valuable, educational content. "Most companies fail because they don't stick with a marketing strategy long enough for it to succeed," he says.

Track and Improve

Here's where the magic (and the money) happens: measurement.

Because let's be honest, if you're not tracking what's working, you're not marketing – you're guessing. While guesswork might occasionally lead to the odd lucky win, it's not a strategy you can scale.

So let's turn your marketing into a machine that not only runs consistently, but also improves over time.

Set Your KPIs

Start with a few core metrics you can measure monthly. Don't overcomplicate it. Just ask:

How many leads came in this month?

Which channels brought them in? (Email? Instagram? Letters?)

What's the cost per lead?

What's the conversion rate from enquiry to instruction?

What's the lifetime value of a client?

How long is the average time between the first touchpoint and instruction?

You don't need a massive CRM to track this (although it helps). A simple spreadsheet will do. What matters is that you measure *something*, and you do it consistently. Think of it like tracking your steps. You won't always hit 10,000, but if you're not counting, you've no idea how close (or far) you are.

Make Data-Led Decisions

Once you have some numbers, the insights follow.

You might discover that your Instagram is generating a lot of engagement, but no actual leads. Meanwhile, those not-soglamorous direct mail letters? They're quietly bringing in your most qualified sellers.

This kind of insight helps you double down on what's working and let go of what's not. It stops you from chasing shiny objects and gives you the clarity to stick with a strategy long enough to see results, which is what Chet Holmes calls "pig-headed discipline."

Remember: Consistency beats creativity. A consistent message, delivered through proven channels, tracked and tweaked monthly, will outperform a scattergun of one-hit wonders every time.

Refine and Repeat

At the end of each month or quarter, review your marketing like you would your sales pipeline. Ask:

What channel is producing the best quality leads?

Where are we wasting time or money?

What message is resonating most?

What needs to be improved, simplified, or systemised?

Treat your marketing like a living, breathing part of your business – because it is. The more attention you give it, the more refined and powerful it becomes.

When you track and improve consistently, your marketing *does* become a system that works without you. It becomes predictable. Sustainable. Scalable.

No more waking up in a cold sweat, wondering where the next instruction is coming from.

Instead, you'll be confidently reviewing your lead flow, tweaking your message and watching your calendar fill up with the kind of clients you actually want to work with.

Shift Your Mindset: You Are a Marketer First

Marketing is not what you do when you have time. It's what creates the time, the freedom and the security you're after.

Michael Port says it best: "You don't wait until you're hungry to start hunting." Consistent marketing isn't a luxury; it's a lifeline. You can't rely on bursts of activity. Instead, you must commit to consistent visibility and value.

Think of marketing like brushing your teeth. You don't do it only when you feel like it; you do it daily to prevent decay.

If you want a high-value, high-impact estate agency, you must think like a business owner and not a hustling agent. The agents who thrive in this space are marketers first, estate agents second. And they've built a machine that generates interest, trust and demand – rain or shine.

Your job isn't to hustle endlessly. It's to build systems that work when you're not. So don't wait until you're quiet to start marketing. Start now, stay consistent and step off the rollercoaster for good!

Build the Machine, then Let it Work for You

This chapter isn't about one bad client. It's about what happens when you stop marketing. And here's what we've learned, the hard way and the smart way: Your job as an estate agent isn't to do everything; it's to build the machine that does everything.

And marketing? That's the machine that never sleeps.

Even when you're swamped with listings, even when your phone is ringing off the hook, the marketing must continue. Because when you stop, your future pipeline stops, too.

When you market consistently, you get to choose your clients. You command your fees. You build a business that feels calm, confident and in flow.

So don't wait for the silence. Don't wait for panic to kick in.

Start now. Stay visible. Always be marketing.

Your dream business depends on it.

Chapter 13
We Need to Talk About Kevin

A Surreal Saga of Lies, £20M and a Masterclass in Gut Instinct and Gullibility

Let's be honest, estate agency would be a lot easier if everyone told the truth, kept their promises and had £20 million sitting neatly in their bank account, ready to go.

But that's not the real world.

In real life, even the most experienced agents sometimes get blindsided by a story so elaborate and so believable that every warning bell in your body starts quietly ringing. Yet, somehow, you still ignore it.

This is the story of one such time.

A time when logic was overruled by hope. When every instinct we had was shouting "no," but we said "maybe." When we learned, in a very expensive and very emotional way, that your gut isn't just there to make you nervous. It's there to save you.

We're sharing this cautionary tale not to scare you. Although honestly, if it makes you a little more paranoid about too-good-to-be-true buyers, that's probably not a bad thing. We're sharing it because this business is built on judgment calls, and sometimes, getting it wrong can cost more than just a lost sale.

This story is messy, a bit painful, occasionally hilarious and absolutely packed with lessons about why trusting your gut isn't a "nice to have." It's a must if you want to build a resilient, high-integrity business.

So grab a coffee (or something stronger – you might need it), and let us tell you about Kevin...

It was a beautiful summer's day, and we had recently launched one of our most expensive listings and fees: £3m at £52,500 – so, we had a lot to prove. Mrs Client was lovely; Mr was short and usually angry. He was a no-nonsense man who didn't like estate agents. Just him telling me this wound me up immensely and drove me to try to prove him wrong! This was mistake number one.

Kevin had arrived to view the home with his girlfriend. I was excited to meet him as we'd spoken at length about the home over the phone when qualifying for the viewing. He was a local man who had dreamed of owning a house along this road, "one with gates," and he was now in a position to do so. He seemed genuinely excited, and so was I.

Neither he nor his car suggested he had the funds to buy such a home, but you can never tell a book by its cover, can you? Your gut instinct, however, should not be ignored!

The house was beautiful, had a huge garden, several acres of woodland, a swimming pool, a tennis court and an annexe above the garage – perfect for the office Kevin wanted to run his new charitable business from. I thought, *This was the buyer!* The only compromise (and there's always one) was that you could clearly hear the dual carriageway, which ran parallel to the home. If it weren't there, then it would be a £4m home! If the price was right, however, then people could look past this for such a "wow" home.

I showed Kevin and his girlfriend around. His excitement was oozing from every pore, and after strolling around the garden, I felt compelled to ask how he planned to fund the purchase (I'm nosy, but I'm also aware of time wasters, not just our legal obligation, and this was a large purchase for anyone!). Kevin stopped and started to tell me the following story. He was very engaging and seemed totally genuine. I was hooked!

In the late 1970s, Kevin lived in London, selling vans to the trade. One day, he was walking down the high street when his path was blocked by several boxes. He noticed a man hurriedly trying to put them into a shabby storefront, and Kevin offered to help as it wasn't an area where you left items unattended for long. They got chatting, and Kevin learned that the man, Singh, had recently arrived from Uganda, where he and his parents were fleeing the persecution of Idi Amin. His dream was to set up his own business (hence all the boxes) and was on the lookout for a van. Well, it just so happened that he was sat talking to a van salesman and a deal was done and a friendship made. They kept in touch over the years, meeting once or twice a year. Kevin introduced him to people he knew in business who could help, and watched as this man's business grew and grew into a household name.

Kevin looked at me, and his eyes filled with tears. He told me how Singh had called him recently to arrange a lunch. During their lunch, Singh recounted how they had met and how much he had appreciated Kevin's help all those years ago. Little did Kevin know back then that, after 45 years, he would be gifted something that would change his life forever. Singh explained that he had made a promise to himself that, thanks to Kevin's support, he would give him 10% of the sale price of his company, which had recently sold for over £200m! Kevin then excitedly produced his mobile phone, accessed his banking app, and even though I wasn't wearing my glasses, I could see over £20m was sat in his account. There were a lot of noughts! I became as emotional as Kevin. I wanted to hug him. In fact, I think I did! I was blown away by the tale, and what a wonderful, generous human being Singh was; it was also heartening to see that there were some amazing people out there. We smiled and walked back to the house, with me feeling a sense of faith had been restored in an often-negative world, but also knowing I'd sold the house!

Now, something I hadn't mentioned before was that this wasn't the first offer we'd received for this home. The first was also to a cash buyer who, due to some market uncertainty, decided that a £250k reduction four weeks after his offer had been accepted would be a reasonable request. "Just in case the home was worth less in a few months' time," he said – so, we binned him off! Naturally, my client was now more nervous (and a little angrier), so we agreed that Kevin would sign an agreement, which meant that if he withdrew from the sale, he would forfeit £30,000. There, everyone was protected: I'd get some of the £30k to cover expenses, my client would get the lion's share and Kevin knew he wouldn't be gazumped. The agreement was for three months. Neither party could withdraw or re-market during this time, as this would be in breach of the agreement.

Solicitors were instructed, a survey was booked and the conveyancing process started.

The survey was all fine, and after a few days, I received an email from Kevin's solicitor to confirm their AML checks had been satisfied. Great! I was playing golf when I found this out and was so relieved, as this is an incredibly important (and legal) step, especially for a large, cash purchase. I think I played better from then on, but even that improvement was short-lived. Bloody game!

Kevin met with the sellers and agreed to buy most of their furniture as he was coming from a small rental – an amber flag. (I've been told on many occasions that an amber flag is the same as a red one! I'm now telling you the same!) They were selling to move abroad and only wanted a small bolt-hole in the UK, so all was working out well.

The weeks passed, and we drew closer to the exchange. Kevin was asked to deposit funds. "No problem," he said. "I'll transfer them over this evening." Checking in the next day, nothing had arrived with the solicitor, which was another amber flag.

"Don't worry. I'm not very computer literate. I tried to transfer over £300k, and my account wouldn't let me do this in one go, and now it's locked me out. I'll speak to them and get it sorted." "You don't have a private banking contact?" I asked. "Nope, just a standard account at the moment," he replied. *A standard account with £20m in it?*, I thought. I'm sure the bank would have been all over him like a rash, stating they'd "look after it" for him. A little alarm bell started to ring, alongside the two amber flags waving away. *Don't worry,* I thought, *he's signed a £30k agreement!*

The next few weeks were frankly ridiculous – believable but also really not – with Kevin's bank account still locked, fraud alerts and the bank needing to conduct its own checks to determine the source of the £20m etc. "I'm going to visit the bank HQ in Birmingham and sort this myself. It's bloody ridiculous," Kevin said. Meanwhile, I'm speaking with my client more than daily as we try to work out if he's legit or not, but then he's signed an insured agreement. What would he gain? Round and around we went. What's he gaining? It's not fraud as no money has changed hands. His story is so out there that it has to be real. Perhaps he's just a lovable idiot struggling to manage a sudden, massive increase in wealth. Let's stick with him; we have the agreement in place and can't re-market anyway or we'd be in breach.

Kevin visited the bank; he called me the following day when I was driving with Lucy. "I got so angry in the bank that I got arrested as I hit the security guard," he informed us.

"You did what?!"

"Yes, I'm sorry. I have a past. I was sent to prison several years ago for assault. When you're released, they give you a bank account which is flagged as it's monitored. With the £20m that's arrived, the bank is asking all sorts of questions and it's going through their own rigorous checks." My brother-in-law has worked for a major bank for years. I asked him about this, and he confirmed that this was more than likely the case. So, we continued on our path, not really knowing where we were going. I was still in disbelief at what I had just heard. I laughed, then grew nervous and scared, but eventually returned to laughing...

The days went by. Kevin would update me with dates that the bank said they would have completed their checks, and these dates came and went. Enough time had passed that the agreement was coming to an end. The parties agreed to extend it by another six months, as we all felt he was genuine but just not managing his affairs well, combined with the banks being "difficult." I mean, who would make up such a story, and the big question is, to what gain?

His solicitor then advised that they could no longer discuss the sales progress with me – another amber flag. There were many waving now, and they were replaced with a huge, massive red one. I reminded his solicitor of the email they had sent me, confirming that their anti-money laundering (AML) checks were fine. They advised me they were checking again but would no longer keep me apprised. This is standard when concerns about money laundering or the source of funds are raised. My heart sank, my body chilled and I felt sick. My poor family took the brunt of my emotions, which I'm still sorry for.

By this stage, Kevin had stated that he'd been to his local bank, which said it'd take a few days to run the necessary checks. He'd been to HQ, apparently hit a security guard, spent the night in the nick, been to hospital with some illness from a holiday and still no sign of the funds or an end date. The only option we were left with was to make a claim against the agreement and secure £30k for my client, with no sale. So, we started this process. Kevin, at this point, is still promising that the funds will be cleared soon.

The claim did go through – it had to be adjudicated by a King's Counsel, and my client was found in favour, receiving the payment. I told Kevin to just stop and move on with his life. He still assured me all would be well. We placed the home back on the market to see if we would be third-time lucky. Interestingly, their neighbour also placed their home on the open market and, within a couple of weeks, went under offer. It was similar in size and price, so I was surprised it went under offer so quickly, especially since the people hadn't viewed our home, which was just next door.

A couple of weeks passed, and I received a phone call from the agent selling the neighbour's home. I congratulated him on finding a buyer so quickly, to which he said that was the reason for the call. He said that the buyer had offered the full asking price but insisted that it be taken off the market and all future viewings be cancelled, which they agreed to do. When they received their proof of funds, they noticed something unusual on a bank statement, and they asked if I could let them know who our buyer had been. He heard that we'd had some issues with a buyer. "A man called Kevin," I said

"Shit!" I heard. "It's him!"

So, our friend Kevin had now walked into the house just next door and started the process all over again. I'll let that sink in. He didn't look at a house in a few miles away, or a neighbouring town, or a different city, location or anything sensible. Oh no, he boldly went next bloody door! I called Kevin, but we've never spoken again, and I've not heard his name since. I wonder what he's up to?

The moral of the story? We still don't know what his goal was or is. It wasn't an attempt at money laundering as there was no money. It couldn't have been fraud as he was never going to get the house as he couldn't buy it. So, was he just a time-waster? A fantasist? Let's not forget, he signed a legal contract for which he's now being pursued for £30k! I do not know what it was all about, but I do know we tried to do the right thing. We put assurances in place, gave people the benefit of the doubt and none of it worked. We lost the instruction and didn't do anything to improve our clients' view of estate agents. Could it happen again? I'd like to think not as the signs were there (we learnt a lot), but I'd worry about an agreement again as this restricts you and your client with re-marketing until it's lapsed. Listen to your gut.

There's a phrase in the estate agency world: Buyers are liars. Now, that's quite a sweeping statement, and it's not typically true. But sometimes, it is, and they are, and only they know why they do it!

Gut Instinct in Business: What Kevin Taught Us

Sometimes in business, logic will give you data, but instinct gives you truth.

Kevin's story was an Oscar-worthy performance – emotional, detailed and even heartwarming! And that was the problem. Because even as we nodded and smiled, something deep down was screaming, *This doesn't feel right!* We heard it. We ignored it. And we paid for it.

Here's what this very expensive, emotionally draining, mildly surreal experience taught us about trusting your gut in business.

Amber Flags Are Red Flags in Disguise

If it walks like a red flag, waves like a red flag and gives you a headache at 2 am – it's a red flag. We told ourselves Kevin's oddities were explainable. But weird is still weird, even when it has a charming backstory and a fake banking app.

Lesson: Trust the pattern, not the performance.

Your Gut Is the Data Point No Spreadsheet Can Give You

Intuition isn't guesswork; it's your subconscious making sense of micro-cues, experience and energy. When something feels off, it usually is. And when you override that feeling with logic, you often regret it.

Lesson: If it doesn't feel right, you don't need a second opinion. You need to pause.

Contracts Can't Compensate for Poor Judgment

Yes, we had a £30k withdrawal clause. Yes, we had legal protection. But did that protect our client's time, stress, trust and emotional energy? Not even close. Legal safety nets are great, but they should never be your Plan A.

Lesson: Don't use paperwork to override common sense.

Desperation Dilutes Discernment

We'd already lost one buyer. We wanted this deal to work. We *needed* it to work. And that clouded our decision-making. We held on far longer than we should have because the pipeline felt thin.

Lesson: Always be marketing so you're never operating from a place of lack. Desperation can lead you to say "yes" to the wrong people.

Be Kind, But Be Clear

Giving someone the benefit of the doubt doesn't mean giving them the keys to your credibility. You can be compassionate without being naive. Boundaries matter.

Lesson: Kindness and clarity are not mutually exclusive.

Your Reputation Is Your Most Valuable Asset

The sad truth is that this saga didn't just cost us time and energy. It risked our reputation with our client. We didn't cause the mess, but we got caught in it. And in this business, perception is everything.

Lesson: Trust isn't earned through transactions. It's preserved through tough calls.

Instinct is there to protect you. Use it. Trust it. Honour it. Because the next time something feels "off," it probably is, and you don't want to be the agent trying to explain Kevin to your clients.

Chapter 14
Selling With Heart: The Clients Who Helped Build Our Business

The Grit, the Grind and the Great: Real-Life Client Stories to Amuse and Inspire You

Michael here with a final word before we end. I hope you've found the anecdotes I've shared throughout this book both useful and entertaining. Every story shared here is a real example of situations we've encountered and had to navigate.

When reviewing the completed manuscript, Lucy and I noticed something: We'd only included stories about the challenges, the difficult clients and the tricky situations. And while those are important to share, we didn't want you, dear reader – someone who's either building a new business or transforming an existing one – to come away thinking that all clients in this sector are difficult. They're not!

Yes, property can be challenging. Buying and selling homes in England isn't always straightforward, especially when you compare it to processes in places like America, Australia or even Scotland, where a transaction can complete in just seven days. However, if you position your business to attract the right kind of clients, this industry can be joyful, fulfilling and full of fantastic people.

So, in the spirit of balance, here are just a few of the wonderful clients we've had the pleasure of working with over the years.

A Thank You to Rhys

When you start any business, you need clients. Rhys was our very first one.

Back in my previous life working in IT, I knew Rhys – a lovely, softly spoken man. Never in a million years did I imagine that, after making a complete career change, he'd be the one to give us our very first instruction.

We founded the business at the end of 2016 and initially partnered with Keller Williams, the American real estate training company. Their training laid the foundations for everything we do today. During one training day, we were asked to call everyone we knew. Essentially, review our contacts like an old-school Rolodex.

When I got to "D" for Dean (another ex-colleague and an all-around cheeky chap; love him to bits), he said, "I think Rhys is trying to sell his home. Give him a call." So, I did.

"Hello Mike," Rhys said, "How are you?" I explained what Lucy and I were doing, and without hesitation, he replied, "Of course you can sell my home. My current agent has been useless." I was gobsmacked.

I went back into the training room and announced, "I've got our first instruction!" The property was a semi-detached, old chapel in Maidenhead, listed at £600k. It was an hour away from us (not ideal), but we were off!

And you know what they say: "For Sale" boards breed more boards. It's true. Thanks to Rhys and the quality of our marketing, even in those early days, we picked up four more homes in Maidenhead. That was a game-changer. It wasn't quite our local patch, but we sold every one of them, giving us much-needed income and invaluable experience.

Eventually, we won a listing in our very own village, and from there, we started growing in the area we'd always intended to serve. But I will never forget what Rhys did for us or the impact it had. That first step was everything.

Thank you, Rhys.

Geoff and Yvonne

We honestly wouldn't be where we are today without Geoff and Yvonne. They are possibly the loveliest couple you could ever meet.

It all started with a cold call Lucy made. They were already on the market with another agent, but a mutual friend tipped us off that they weren't happy. Lucy was nervous about calling them. This was early in our business journey, and their home was worth £1m. At that time, we hadn't even listed – let alone sold – a property of that value. Plus, cold calling wasn't in Lucy's comfort zone. But she took a deep breath, put on her "big girl pants" and made the call.

To her surprise, Geoff was incredibly welcoming. Lucy booked a meeting and we were over the moon.

When we arrived to meet them, they couldn't have been more gracious. Both were retired, and they were warm and engaging. As a bonus, their home was stunning. They loved our approach, and by the end of the meeting, they signed with us on the spot. Our first million-pound listing! We were beyond thrilled.

Of course, even beautiful homes have compromises. In this case, the garden wasn't huge. But thanks to our tailored marketing strategy, we secured two offers and agreed on a sale at the full asking price within weeks. We were all ecstatic.

What we didn't know then was that Geoff had a nickname: "Stamp Duty Geoff." They had a habit of moving every couple of years. And sure enough, they've moved four times since. Each time, we were the only agent they called.

Over time, they've become more than clients – they've become friends. We catch up over lunch now and again, and while they seem to have finally settled down, we'll always be grateful to them for helping launch us into the prime property market.

Mark and Vanessa

Next up, Mark and Vanessa. Wow, what a duo!

Mark rang Lucy one day to book a viewing on a unique apartment we were marketing. He was considering it as a potential development project. Mark is a seasoned Independent Financial Adviser (IFA) and a property developer, and this particular property had caught his eye. After what turned into a long and lively call (Mark loves a good chat and has a wealth of fascinating stories), a viewing was arranged. Off I went to meet him.

The apartment turned out not to be the right fit, but something even better came from it: a friendship.

Mark and his wife, Vanessa, owned a plot of land with planning permission for an 8,000 sq. ft. home, which they wanted to sell as is. They asked us to handle the sale, and we did, quickly and successfully. That was just the beginning.

Next, they'd just completed the stunning restoration of two historic cottages in Oxford. We listed and sold both for well over the asking price. Then came a development in Bideford, North Devon: 10 beautiful homes, each with charm and quality. They entrusted us to sell those as well, and we are currently doing so. In fact, we even bought one ourselves. They're that good!

Mark and Vanessa have become true partners in every sense of the word. They've supported us during tough times, offered financial guidance, helped some of our clients with equity release and estate planning and, more than anything, they've become dear friends. We're even going on holiday together soon.

This friendship, this collaboration, feels like just the beginning.

Peter and Louise

Then there's Peter and Louise, buyers of a home we were selling at the time for £1.75m, which was a huge deal for us back then.

The seller was a lovely man who had built the house for his wife, but heartbreakingly, she passed away shortly after its completion. He couldn't bear to live there without her and wanted to move on to start fresh. Naturally, we were committed to getting him the best return possible.

The sale took a little time. The house had striking curb appeal, but the interiors were quite bespoke to the seller's taste, something not everyone could envision living with. Enter Peter and Louise. They had incredible vision, loved the potential and agreed to buy at the full asking price.

On completion day, I met the seller away from the property, as it was too emotional for him. We shared a hug, he shed a tear and set off for a smallholding on the south coast to begin his next chapter.

Peter and Louise were buzzing. As a thank-you, they gave me two beautiful bottles of wine and excitedly talked through their renovation plans. A year later, they invited us back to see the transformation. It was breathtaking. They had added a stunning garden room, redesigned the kitchen, updated all the bathrooms and en-suites and redecorated the entire home. It was jaw-droppingly beautiful.

They mentioned they might sell at some point, and that if they did, they wanted us to handle it, despite their son working for a major corporate estate agency. They believed in our marketing touch and trusted us with the home's story.

Six months later, the property was back on the market, and this time for £2.75 million. They had invested a lot into it, and it truly was worth every penny. We didn't have to wait long to find the perfect buyers, as another wonderful couple came along. The woman instantly fell in love, particularly with the kitchen, which happened to be by the same company as her current one.

The only hiccup? They hadn't yet listed their own home. Luckily, they were in a position to proceed without selling, but understandably, preferred not to.

Peter and Louise, being the brilliant humans they are, agreed to accept the offer at full asking price, giving the buyers a fixed amount of time to sell, on the condition that if they didn't, the sale would proceed independently.

The buyers asked us to handle their sale as well, and we listed their home at £2 million. Another beautiful property and another great match made. Within three months, keys were exchanged and both couples were happily settled into their new homes.

And just like that, we'd closed a £4.75 million deal with grace, joy and two fantastic experiences.

Looking Back

These stories remind us that property isn't just about listings, negotiations and transactions. It's about people. Real, genuine, brilliant people. From Geoff and Yvonne's unwavering loyalty to Mark and Vanessa's inspiring partnership to Peter and Louise's generosity and trust. These clients not only shaped our business but also became part of our lives.

Yes, there are challenging clients in every industry. But when you attract the right ones, this business becomes more than a career; it becomes a series of shared successes, human moments and lasting relationships.

And that's what makes it all worth it.

Conclusion:
This Is Just the Beginning

Let's take a moment, shall we?

You made it. You've powered through mindset shifts, marketing machines, messy negotiations and more client stories than your local pub's landlord. You've survived "Feast and Famine," faced the perils of Kevin and hopefully circled "Amber Flag = Red Flag" in bold on your notes. Bravo!

This book wasn't written to be read; it was written to be *used*. If your highlighter has run dry and you've got at least three pages dog-eared beyond repair, then we've done our job. And if you're reading this in your slippers with a G&T in hand while muttering, "Yes, *this* is the kind of business I want," then consider this your official nudge: Now's the time to build it.

So, what have we actually learned?

Let's Recap: What Elite Agents Know

You Are Not Here to Serve Everyone

You are not the say-yes-to-everything agent. You're here for the right clients: the Radiators, not the Drains. You're here to work with people who value you, not haggle you down like you're flogging socks at a market stall.

Mindset Is Not Fluff, It's Fuel

You've learned to think like a business owner, not a busy fool. You've seen how beliefs drive behaviour and how behaviour builds a business. Confidence isn't optional; it's the currency of trust.

You Need to Know Who You're Talking To

Ideal Client Avatars aren't just marketing fluff. They're the difference between a thriving business and one powered by caffeine and resentment.

Lead Generation Isn't Something You Do When You're Desperate

If you only market when you're quiet, you'll never get off the rollercoaster. Always. Be. Marketing. Even when you're busy. *Especially* when you're busy.

The Listing Appointment Is Not an Audition

It's a two-way interview. You're not trying to win every instruction; you're trying to find the right partnerships.

Luxury Never Goes on Sale (And Neither Do You)

Value-led conversations trump cheap fees. And if someone doesn't "get" what you're worth, they're not your person. Full stop.

Bespoke Marketing Isn't Optional in Premium Homes

You're not in the copy-paste business. You're in the "make them stop scrolling and fall in love" business.

Communication Is Your Secret Weapon

Even if there's no news, let them know. No news *is* news. Silence loses clients. Consistent contact earns trust.

You're a Ninja Negotiator Now

You don't flinch. You lead. You don't chase the highest offer; you evaluate the *right* offer. Calm is contagious. Confidence closes.

You Can Build a Joyful Business – With Boundaries

This doesn't have to be a grind. When you market consistently, attract the right people, charge what you're worth and protect your energy, this work becomes fun. Yes, fun!

And Then There Was Kevin...

Ah yes. Kevin.

He deserves his own Netflix docuseries. But while his tale was bonkers (seriously, who walks next door and tries it all again?), it gifted us a priceless lesson: Trust your gut. Contracts are great, but instincts are golden. If something feels off, it probably is. You don't need to be cynical, but you do need to be savvy.

Kevin was a plot twist. But Geoff and Yvonne, Mark and Vanessa, Peter and Louise? They were the proof that this industry, when done right, is bursting with brilliance. People who become friends. Clients who become raving fans. Stories that stay with you long after the keys have changed hands.

What's Next?

We didn't write this book so you could finish it and say, "Nice read." We wrote it so you could finish it and say, "Right. Let's do this."

And if you want to maintain that momentum, we'd love to support you. You don't have to do this alone.

Here's how you can stay connected with us and continue your Elite Agent journey:

Own Your Patch: Become a Stowhill Estates Franchisee

Join our growing network of Elite Agents who are building their own empires under the Stowhill brand. We provide you with the tools, support, marketing and brand power, so you can focus on selling beautiful homes and running a business you love.

Learn more at stowhillestates.com

Join Our Mastermind Community: The Elite Agent Collective

Access expert training, live Q&As, masterclasses and a like-minded crew of agents who are all raising the bar in the industry. Whether you're brand new or already flying, this is the rocket fuel you need to level up.

Check it out at eliteagentcollective.com.

Work 1:1 With Lucy

Want personalised support from someone who's been there, done it and still does it daily? Lucy offers limited private coaching spots for ambitious agents who are ready to move fast and dive deep.

Apply at lucyjoerincoaching.com.

Download Your Resources From This Book

Visit www.eliteagentcollective.com/resources to download all the resources mentioned in this book or scan the QR code below for quick access.

Your Final Pep Talk

You don't need a fancy car, 20 years of experience or a silver tongue. You need a strategy. A system. A bit of courage. And the belief that you can do this differently.

If we can do it, sitting at our kitchen table with no listings, no experience, no clue – then so can you.

This is not the end. This is your beginning.

Now go out there, find your dream clients, sell some beautiful homes and show this industry exactly how good estate agency *can* be.

We're rooting for you.

With grit and gratitude,

Lucy & Michael
The Elite Agent Collective

Elite Agent Reading & Resource List

For the Agent Who Wants to Go Further, Faster

Whether you're ready to build a marketing machine, negotiate like a Ninja or avoid the next Kevin, you'll find something here to deepen your learning, sharpen your skills and keep you inspired.

Estate Agency & Real Estate-Specific Books

The Selective Estate Agent by Sam Ashdown

A brilliant guide for agents who want to stop chasing every instruction and instead attract higher-value listings with ease. If you enjoyed our take on "dream clients only," you'll love this.

The Millionaire Real Estate Agent by Gary Keller

A must-read for agents who want to understand the systems, models, and mindset behind building a scalable, sustainable business. Part practical manual, part mindset shift.

Sell It Like Serhant by Ryan Serhant

Energetic, entertaining, and full of real-world advice from one of the most well-known luxury agents in the world. Great for learning how to build a standout personal brand.

Fear Is Just a Four-Letter Word by Tracy Tutor

A fierce and empowering read from one of LA's top female agents. Confidence, boundaries, and high-stakes negotiations—this one hits all the right notes.

Exactly What to Say: For Real Estate Agents
by Phil M. Jones & Chris Smith

Script-based advice for powerful, persuasive conversations. Ideal if you want to sharpen your language without sounding like a script-reading robot.

Your Best Life in Real Estate by Debbie De Grote

Helps agents avoid burnout and build a business that supports their life, not runs it.

The Honest Real Estate Agent by Mario Jannatpour

Especially helpful for newer agents. A values-led approach to winning business and serving clients well.

Mindset & Personal Growth Books

The Big Leap *by Gay Hendricks*

Break through your upper limits and step into your "Zone of Genius."

The Chimp Paradox *by Dr. Steve Peters*

Understand your inner "chimp" brain and how to manage it in high-stress moments.

The Slight Edge *by Jeff Olson*

How small daily disciplines lead to massive success.

Business Strategy & Entrepreneurship Books

The E-Myth Revisited *by Michael E. Gerber*

Build a business that works for you, not just because of you.

Built to Sell *by John Warrillow*

Turn your agency into a business that's not just profitable, but potentially sellable.

Atomic Habits *by James Clear*

The definitive guide to habit formation and long-term behaviour change.

Marketing & Branding Books

This Is Marketing by Seth Godin

Generous, consistent, trust-building marketing explained by one of the best in the biz.

Book Yourself Solid by Michael Port

Learn how to fill your pipeline with the right clients, sustainably.

No B.S. Direct Marketing by Dan Kennedy

Tough love advice on how to market effectively and measurably.

The Ultimate Sales Machine by Chet Holmes

A brilliant guide to dominating your niche with consistency and discipline.

Negotiation & Influence Books

Never Split the Difference by Chris Voss

Learn negotiation from an ex-FBI hostage negotiator. Tactical empathy is your new secret weapon.

Influence: The Psychology of Persuasion by Robert Cialdini

Understand what drives human behaviour and how to guide decision-making ethically.

Podcasts & Online Learning

Elite Agent Collective (www.eliteagentcollective.com)

Our community and training hub for ambitious agents ready to scale smart.

Ignite Your Estate Agency

With Sam Ashdown and Phil Jones of Ashdown Jones

The Tim Ferriss Show **(Chris Voss episodes in particular)**

Packed with mindset, performance and negotiation gold.

Tom Ferry Podcast Experience

US real estate guru on marketing, mindset and modern estate agency.

The Diary of a CEO **by** *Steven Bartlett*

World-class conversations on entrepreneurship, branding and personal growth.

Tools We Love

Canva Pro for beautiful social graphics, listing brochures and brand assets.

Mailchimp / ActiveCampaign are great for email automation and nurturing.

The Marketing Autopilots for super cool WhatsApp automation

Later / Buffer / Metricool to plan and schedule content without last-minute stress

Trello / ClickUp / Notion to stay on top of listings, marketing and team tasks

Want More?

Download your resources from this book through <u>www. eliteagentcollective.com/resources</u> or scan the QR code below.

Private Coaching with Lucy at <u>lucyjoerincoaching.com</u>

Own your patch with Stowhill Estates at <u>stowhillestates.com</u>

Join The Elite Agent Collective at <u>eliteagentcollective.com</u>

Let this be your library, your launchpad and your permission slip to go big. You've got this!

www.ingramcontent.com/pod-product-compliance
Lightning Source LLC
Chambersburg PA
CBHW071322210326
41597CB00015B/1308